THE PARLOUR REBELLION

Isabel Bassett

THE PARLOUR REBELLION

Profiles in the Struggle for Women's Rights

McClelland and Stewart Limited

0-7710-1096-6

The Canadian Publishers
McClelland and Stewart Limited
25 Hollinger Road, Toronto

Contents

To my husband, John,
for his uncompromising belief in the freedom and dignity of the
individual, regardless of race, creed, nationality — or sex.

Preface

Most Canadians know nothing about the women in their country's history. If pushed, a few might recall Laura Secord, for years our one national heroine, or Susannah Moodie, whose writings on her pioneer experiences in Canada are currently enjoying a revival. While most people know something about Emmeline Pankhurst and her suffragettes in England, and about the stars of the present wave of women's lib – Betty Friedan, Germaine Greer, and Gloria Steinem – we remain oblivious to the fact that since 1800 Canadian women have been fighting for and in some cases achieving the rights and privileges enjoyed by men. How many, for example, have heard of Judge Emily Murphy and her historic battle to change the legal status of Canadian women to "persons" so that they would be eligible to sit in the Canadian Senate? Who remembers Nellie McClung and her role in the fight for women's suffrage in Manitoba and Alberta? And how many of the thousands of women who attend university in Canada have heard of Maude Abbott's struggle to get into McGill Medical School in Quebec in the early 1890's, or of Helen MacGill's battle for admittance to university in Toronto in the 1880's? These women and others broke out of the restricted sphere allotted to them and rebelled against the conventions of their times to achieve many of the rights Canadian women enjoy today, including the rights to vote, to attend university, to enter the professions, and to hold political office.

None of these, of course, came easily. For approximately one hundred years, from 1840 to 1940, when all Canadian women at last had the right to vote provincially and federally, these women were engaged in a long and difficult confrontation with society. The battle began when some Canadian women decided to seek alternatives to the conventional roles prescribed for members of their sex, by attempting to enter previously male-dominated fields such as educational institutions and the professions. Although few of these women were concerned about women's rights at the outset of their careers, the restrictions and prejudices they encountered and the injustices they witnessed led many to devote their lives to crusading for women's rights. They soon discovered, however, that by venturing outside the prescribed order of things they challenged the sacred tenets in their society. Violating these required uncommon courage and determination. Like all pioneers, they suffered humiliations, disappointments, and defeat. And like their ancestors who toiled to clear the land of the forests, these women worked to clear the prejudices that denied women the freedom to lead a more fulfilling life. Individually, their efforts made few inroads; collectively, they opened the way for change and growth in our society.

As sheer entertainment, the stories of these early champions of women's rights read like fiction: they were determined, almost heroic protagonists who battled formidable foes. These stories, however, are true records of heroism and form a vital part of the history of this country. The hundred years of struggle – from 1840 to 1940 – witnessed woman's liberation from the female ghetto of the nineteenth century and saw her win the vote – that symbolic passport to freedom in our political system without which no individual is truly free to participate in the shaping of his – or her – destiny. This account is a heartfelt tribute to the key figures in the struggle.

Acknowledgements

I would like to thank Clara Thomas, professor of English at York University, for giving me the idea of writing this book and for encouraging me along the way; Catherine Price, for her early and valuable suggestions about the manuscript; and Joanne Blackwell, who so willingly typed and retyped these pages over the past year and a half, and who helped in some of the research as well. Finally, I want to thank my husband, John, for his sustained and genuine interest in my work despite the inconveniences it has sometimes caused him.

Helen Gregory MacGill (1864-1947) as a young socialite. She later became one of the first women admitted to a Canadian university.

CHAPTER ONE

The Way They Were

At the middle of the last century, Canadian women were not legally regarded as "persons" under the British North America Act. Nor, for that matter were they treated as such, for under the laws of the time they had few more rights than animals. They had no vote in federal, provincial, or municipal elections; they had no property rights, and they had no rights to their own children. They were barred from attending Canadian universities and from entering professions such as law and medicine. And although school boards began hiring women teachers in the 1840's to meet a shortage of male staff, the step caused such a public outcry that provincial governments had to limit the number of women teachers hired by any one board. Yet most women in Canada did not object, publicly at least, to their lot.

Women pioneers who settled the Canadian backwoods had to pour all their time and energy into establishing a home and a new life for their families. They had more than enough to do, without taking on the task of challenging their role as homemakers. In their case at least, this role was almost inevitable, given the nature of pioneer life. The division of labour between the sexes was determined by the physical capabilities of each: a man's strength was needed to clear the land; a woman's to prepare food and clothing and bear and raise the children who, in themselves, were an economic necessity for farmers at the time.

Anna Leveridge's letters to her mother in England tell of the work involved in creating a new life in the remote area of Hastings County, Ontario, in the 1880's. Her story reflects that of countless other immigrants and, more particularly, the plight of the women among them. To begin with, the physical discomforts and hardships confronting a settler's wife were almost too numerous to bear. They took their toll, both physically and mentally. Anna soon came to see the inclement weather as some uncontrollable force bent on creating suffering and toil. In winter the family coped as best they could, huddling together for warmth at night and stuffing the windows with rags. But the summer, instead of bringing longed-for relief, brought only unbearable heat, tormenting mosquitoes, and long hours of work. "You would have thought the children had measles," Anna wrote despairingly to her mother, "they were so bitten when the black flies were so bad." At times the land itself seemed to be the settlers' chief adversary, conspiring against their efforts to clear the fields. The Leveridges found to their dismay that no sooner had they cleared a field than "enormous ferns shot up from roots which had not been completely removed and young tree growth emerged...as the forest tried to renew itself."

Since nothing was ready-made in their new land, pioneer women had to adjust to new techniques and processes just to feed and clothe themselves. "They spin their own wool, also they make their own sugar, [and] kill their own meat," Anna noted, dismayed at first by the workload ahead of her. Nonetheless, in time she became as expert as the more experienced settlers at these and other tasks. She found it more difficult, however, to adjust mentally to a life so far away from a church, school, shop, or post office. Like many other Anglo-Saxon settlers, Anna had been accustomed in England to such facilities as libraries, concerts, and newspapers, not to mention schools. Until the new school was built, she decried the fact that her children were being deprived of a proper education. Despite these difficulties, women like Anna gradually adapted to and learned to love their new country. Many even came to enjoy the challenge of attaining their dream of providing a home for their family, elusive as it sometimes seemed. Moreover, as members of a small community, they learned to work together to achieve common goals.

While Canadian women living in rural areas struggled with the physical and mental problems that grew out of their attempt to combat a seemingly hostile universe, upper- and middle-class women living in towns faced another kind of adversary – society. The class factor is significant here. Women of the working classes were more or less "liberated" in spite of themselves. They were forced for economic reasons to go to work at an early age, just as their mothers and grandmothers had done before them. In contrast, women in the upper classes had plenty of free time to become frustrated and discontented. Since their husbands and fathers prospered economically and could afford servants, these women's lives consisted of an endless round of entertaining the "right people," calling on friends and relatives, and filling in time with gossip. It was the "same old routine every day," commented one bored young lady of the times in her diary. "I think it might do as well to write one day and copy all the rest down from it, there is so little variety." It was, however, difficult for them to change the monotonous pattern. Victorian and Edwardian society carefully prepared all women but those of the lower classes for the role of hostess, wife, and mother – in that order. In the case of the upper classes in particular, training for girls laid far more stress on the cultivation of social graces than on the practical skills of homemaking. "We were trained for every kind of social function, especially a royal drawing-room, as most of the girls hoped to be presented at Court" was how Martha Black described her education during the seventies and eighties. "I danced, played and sang a little, recited, did fine needlework, painted china and water-colour pictures, made 'wonderful' lemon cream pies, angel food and salad dressing...I knew how to dress for and act at receptions, dinner-parties, musicals and dances." With such training, Martha was considered ready for the career of wife and mother, although, as she pointed out years later, she was, in fact, educated for neither.

Just as this impractical education placed limitations on girls, so did the Victorian stress on morality. Martha Black recalls that every precaution was taken to ensure a woman's virtue before marriage: "How we girls of the '70's and '80's were protected. Arriving at South Bend, five miles from the school, we were met at the trains by 'Old Man Shickey,' who watched us like the Sisters. He hustled us into his carriage-hack and never left us until he had delivered us to the Mother Superior." The Sisters checked any attempts to carry on an unchaperoned correspondence by insisting on reading all the girls' mail, only occasionally allowing them to send a private letter to their parents.

As Laura Berton points out, in the early 1900's girls were brought up to think that every able-bodied man was just waiting to seduce them. Raised on such beliefs, women understandably suffered from a host of fears and built-in constraints that curbed their initiative. They were taught that the role of women was to be submissive, docile, Christian mothers, wives, and hostesses. Sermons extolling the virtues of certain women in the community helped to establish definite ideas about what was and was not proper, godly, Christian, and virtuous in women. The standards set by such paragons of virtue were held up as desirable ideals for other members of society. The Reverend Robert Wilson confessed that his booklet, *Piety Portrayed in the Lives of Mr. and Mrs. Burpee*, aimed "to provide a detailed account of an exemplary life upon which others can pattern their behaviour." Throughout this account he emphasized the important part that Mrs. Burpee's virtues played in the family's achievements and status in the community. An obedient, god-fearing wife and mother, Phoebe Elizabeth Burpee (1797-1870) obeyed her husband in all things, even to the extent of converting to his faith despite her own life-long allegiance to the Methodist Church. Mrs. Burpee was also attentive to her duties as wife and mother – roles in which she revealed a complete selflessness, frequently sacrificing her own desires or ideals for the good of her family.

There were numerous other such sermons and booklets on ideal women in nineteenth-century Canadian society, all of which can be seen as an attempt to mould women's ideas, and those of society in general, to adhere to certain prescribed standards of behaviour. This strong arm of society was, in effect, one of the fiercest adversaries that a woman of an independent frame of mind had to reckon with. As one man put it, women were doomed to a "dreary, aimless, brainless, round of exhausting frivolity." But, however pampered and protected from the realities of life and from undesirable influences these girls were, and however much they were conditioned to conform, some of them sensed the rich potential of human experience and were tormented by the narrowness of the life foisted upon them. "I will never acknowledge," said one, "that to get up in the morning, dress prettily, and dawdle through the forenoon with the help of some self-imposed task of needlework, and spend the afternoon in an aimless walk, will make any woman contented."

For the most part, though, women confided such feelings only to their diaries. Indeed, diary-writing provided an important emotional outlet for frustrated women of the nineteenth century, but its potential as a social weapon was exploited only by later generations. Only recently have we learned how bored young Sophia Macnab was with her existence in Hamilton society. She used to wonder what she would do without her diary, which she called her "greatest diversion." And only from her diaries and letters do we know how novelist Lucy Maud Montgomery really felt about her role as a minister's wife. In 1920, she wrote of sitting up late at a young farmer's wedding reception, where "my back, head, mind and soul ached," discussing hen's eggs, new babies, the high cost of living, "and all the other entrancing subjects of 'conversation' in the presence of the minister's wife." And only in the private sanctums of her diary did Julia Lambert remove the cheerful mask she had worn all day as "helpful aunt" in her invalid sister's house and disclose the bitter truth about the life of a spinster, that single ladies were of no consequence and were valuable "only as far as they [could] be useful to others. [At least] those who have husbands to take care of or to be taken care of by them are of some importance at home...[as] they have duties to perform and a station in life to fill."

These women tried in many ways, consciously or unconsciously, to alleviate the monotonous and oppressive routine of their daily lives. In addition to diary-writing, many enjoyed intermittent lapses into ill-health that made them the centre of attention and gossip. In some instances, of course, as in the case of the tubercular Lady Macnab, this preoccupation with their health was fully justified. Generally speaking, however, obsessive concern with health was due to the romantic view of illness fashionable in the nineteenth century. A woman's beauty and femininity were held to be enhanced by ill-health and mysterious ailments, which in turn enhanced the masculinity of the man by casting him in the role of sustainer and protector. Many women cultivated a pale and helpless look in order to solicit the appropriate response from their suitors. Women's preoccupation with illness can also be seen as a defence mechanism against the sexual advances of their husbands. In view of the high death rate from childbirth at the time, it is hardly surprising that many women feared the repercussions of the sexual act. With abstention as the only reliable form of birth control, it seems very likely that women feigned ill-health to ensure their safety and longevity. Such forms of escapism contributed to a growing undercurrent of discontent that steadily gathered strength as the century progressed. It was only a matter of time before this discontent would sweep some women beyond the limits laid down for them and out into the Victorian, sexist, colonial, and regional milieu of nineteenth-century Canada.

Anna Gaudin (1865-1940), who served as a nurse with the Northern Cree in Manitoba for thirty-nine years.

CHAPTER TWO

Missionary Work:
The Earliest Form of Escape

In view of the many frustrations nineteenth-century women had to face, one cannot help wondering whether some of the women who went into missionary work did so to escape the humdrum existence of a housewife, even if the option involved danger, loneliness, and a difficult life in primitive conditions. However, although these women may well have escaped the monotony and dependence of their more conventional role at home, they soon found they had to face a very different set of adversities.

Mary MacKay of Pictou, Nova Scotia, set off for India in 1888. On the boat, she met her husband-to-be, a fellow missionary. She married him upon her arrival, and together they set out for Ujjain. From then on, the young Mrs. Mary Buchanan found her dreams of spreading the gospel thwarted by disease, deformity, filth, crime, violence, and ignorance. As time passed, she encountered enough obstacles in her personal life to force a less resolute and devout person to give up and go home. Her second child, a girl, died of dysentery at fifteen months; the family lived at a subsistence level through famines; and her children faced continual dangers. However, she continued to teach the Bible to the Bihls (the natives of the area) and do what she could to help the sick at the same time as she raised her own family. She was also plagued by illness herself and her health deteriorated year by year until she was forced to remain home in Canada for a time at the end of a sabbatical. She returned to India in due course, only to die within a year, after having spent forty-seven years in India.

The missionaries in outposts across Canada endured as great hardships as those of missionaries in the foreign service. Elizabeth McDougall, the wife of a Methodist missionary in various Canadian Indian settlements before the turn of the century, got her first taste of danger as a bride. One of her husband's responsibilities in the border town where they lived was to confiscate illegal cargoes of liquor from bootleggers, a task that repaid him with many scars from broken bottles wielded by lawbreakers seeking vengeance. Since tribal wars used to flare up and subside without warning, the fate of Mrs. McDougall and their five children, especially during her husband's frequent absences, was always precarious. Moreover, like many early pioneers and missionaries, she lost first a child and then her husband.

Difficult and demanding as these missionaries' lives were, they aroused the imaginations of young girls whose future promised nothing but servitude in the home. The young and beautiful Mary Matheson willingly accepted a marriage proposal that included having "to share...the labours and the perils...of missionary life" in a foreign posting.

This zeal to do something worthwhile, despite the hardships, was far from unique. "I never felt anything of the interest in missionary labor before that I do now...We hear so much about the work," wrote Amelia Johnson to her mother in 1869, after attending a lecture by a woman missionary who had taught for several years in the American South. In the same letter Miss Johnson indicated that she was fully aware of the sacrifices involved:

There is an almost complete isolation from society, and as the northern teacher is looked upon with contempt by all the whites of any standing, he, or she, has to endure a species of social ostracism. One lady, after teaching in a certain town for ten years, said, that in all that time she had not spoken to a single white person save the clerk of the post office.

This is not to say, of course, that the only reason women went into missionary work was a desire to escape their humdrum lives at home. These women did have a genuine desire to be of service to others, and many were deeply religious. Perhaps only unconsciously, religion became a form of escape and a source of fulfilment in their otherwise dreary lives.

Despite its obvious hardships, missionary work had the decided advantage of being one of the few acceptable outlets for a woman's ambitions. Parents rarely objected to a daughter's decision to undertake mission work, either at home or abroad. In fact, some mothers – including Mary MacKay's mother – promised to "give" one of their children to the mission service. Mrs. MacKay realized the difficulties and dangers that lay before her daughter but nevertheless sent Mary to college and then to the university in Toronto where she was registered in Trinity as one of the first women students in the Faculty of Medicine. Such parents, it seemed, took comfort and pride in the knowledge that their child had sacrificed herself for her religion – a fact which also served to enhance their status in the community.

This trend was not restricted to Protestant women nor to one part of the country. Roman Catholic women found a comparable outlet for frustrated ambition in the convent. Though to a modern reader, convent life is almost synonymous with authoritarianism, it had obvious attractions for the nineteenth-century woman, who had little but drudgery and child-bearing to look forward to if she belonged to the lower classes, and nothing more than child-bearing and managing a household if she belonged to the upper classes. In the early days of French

Canada, Indian women understood this only too well. In a contemporary account one writer notes: "Several [Indian girls] announced their intentions to be nuns when they grew up – quick to observe, no doubt, that 'the virgin sisters,' as the Indians called the nuns, were not mere beasts of burden as were their own mothers. They worked hard but, belonging to God, they belonged in a special sense to themselves."

Whether they became Roman Catholic nuns or Protestant missionaries, these women usually gave up a life of comparative ease in exchange for some degree of freedom from family and social restrictions and the hope to find some kind of personal fulfilment. Many, like Anna Gaudin, saw missionary work both as a means of escape and an opportunity to put the skills they had to some useful purpose.

Anna Gaudin

Samuel Gaudin realized the enormity of his request when he asked Anna Young to marry him and "share the life he had chosen for himself in God's service." After four years as a teacher-missionary among the Indians in the remote areas of northern Manitoba, he knew what life was like in the North and that he was demanding that she "go with him to the very ends of the earth, to share...isolation 700 miles from any kind of life to which she had been accustomed, with no doctor nearer than those long miles, with mail at the most not more than four times in the entire year...with no radio, no telegraph [and no] visitors." Anna, however, accepted. Not only was Samuel one of the few people who understood her longing to be more than a mere housewife, but she recognized that she was being offered a unique opportunity to practise her profession as a nurse and serve God in a land where she would be the only trained medical person within hundreds of miles.

Born in 1865 at Oak Point, Quebec, on a farm bordering the Restigouche River, Anna grew up in humble circumstances. Most of her time had been spent helping out around the house and visiting relatives. She was only fifteen when her father died but unquestioningly she took over many of the heavy physical chores on the farm – something that was considered unusual for a girl at that time. "She would harness and hitch up a horse and go into the woods and bring home a load of wood alone," one of her family told her husband later. When her brother arrived home from where he had been working to run the farm, Anna took a job in a country store to gain some measure of independence for herself. Later, while nursing an old lady, Anna decided that she wanted to work in some area of social service. When she learned that the Protestant Episcopal Hospital in Philadelphia accepted and trained girls as nurses she applied and was accepted, despite the objections of her family and friends.

In 1889, nursing schools were still very much a novelty in North America; the first school for nursing had started in 1873 in the United States, and in Canada a year later. There were still a limited number of these schools and they had produced only a few graduates to change public opinion about nurses. Most people still thought of nurses as being tough and dirty, a view supported by one doctor's comments on the Montreal General Hospital around that time:

> Age and frowsiness seemed the chief attributes of the nurse who was ill-educated and was often made more unattractive by the vinous odor of her breath. Cleanliness was not a feature either of the nurse, the ward or the patient; each did as best pleased her and the "langwidge" was frequently painful and free. Armies of rats frequently disported themselves about the wards, and picked up stray scraps left by the patients and sometimes attacked the patients themselves.

Many similar conditions persisted when Anna started the two year nursing training course in Philadelphia in 1889 – only two years after the school had been started. Much later in life she told her husband about other difficulties she had confronted as a student nurse, difficulties which included the work that began at six A.M. and did not end until eight P.M. and the nurses' quarters with their hard beds, constant drafts, dirt, and rats. Nurses received an "allowance" of eight dollars a month during the first year and ten during the second. In spite of this and her loneliness at being separated from her family for the first time, Anna was determined to prove her point and stuck to her work. In a few months, she was appointed head nurse over her ward.

For the next six years she worked in the United States, first as Superintendent of the Women's Surgical Hospital in Philadelphia and then as Matron of the Children's Hospital in the same city. In 1890, when she was visiting some relatives in Long Island during a holiday, Anna first met Samuel Gaudin, one of her many cousins. Although no one seems to remember the details of their romance, the couple apparently became good friends almost immediately. "To her I first confided the story of my application for the Indian work," Samuel later wrote in his autobiography, *Forty-Four Years with the Northern Cree.* Samuel Gaudin was born in 1861, one of eight children of English-speaking parents descended from Huguenot stock who had been converted to Methodism in John Wesley's day. As a young man, he had taught school for seven years in Ontario before going into the ministry in 1889. The summer he met Anna he had just graduated and had answered an advertisement in the church newspaper for a teacher at an Indian school in the Rossville Mission, Norway House, Keewatin in northern Manitoba. When at last, late in August, he received news of his appointment, he bade farewell to his family and Anna Young and headed north.

Although the couple corresponded, it was not until the summer of 1894, when Samuel was on leave again, that he proposed. Immediately after their engagement, however, Samuel had to return to his remote mission post. On his arrival, his superiors sent him 300 miles further north to the isolated Nelson House Mission where, except for two or three letters, he had no contact with Anna for an entire year. That winter Anna could not find a job as a nurse near her home, so she enrolled in the Whitby Ladies' College where she studied china painting, embroidery, and sewing. At least one of these skills was to prove invaluable in the North for, according to her daughter, Esther Ross, her sewing talents later "enabled the family to have curtains on windows, new clothes, and many other items that were impossible to get in the North or were too costly for a missionary's family." At the end of the winter, Anna began packing for her new life, taking special care over the satin wedding dress she had had made in New Jersey.

On her trip to the North, Anna got her first taste of the adventure and physical hardships she would be facing for the rest of her life. She took the train as far as Selkirk, a lumber town on the Red River some twenty miles north of Winnipeg, then boarded the *Red River*, a converted barge, for the twelve-day journey to Warren's Landing at the northern tip of Lake Winnipeg. There was no regular passenger accommodation but the crew gave up their rooms in the pilot house, which Anna shared with a half-breed girl also going North. Conditions were rather primitive and passengers were expected to cook their own meals on a rusty wood-stove braced on deck. Anna soon discovered this could be more than just inconvenient for on windy days she spent her time dodging the smoke that belched out of the short stove-pipe. However, she soon adjusted to the inconveniences and began questioning two ministers on board about the people and life in the North. When the conductor had helped her off the train in Selkirk, he had said, "I can't say that I envy you your trip to the North...I hope that your young man is worth it." The two ministers now told her that only two boats a year managed to get into her husband's district – in June and September – for the early freeze-up restricted all travel to dog-sled for the rest of the winter. This statement brought home to Anna the reality of her impending isolation as nothing else had.

Samuel was to meet her at Warren's Landing for the last and most difficult part of the journey. Anna had not seen her fiancé for almost a year but, as nineteenth-century propriety did not permit them to kiss in public, after a formal greeting they climbed into Samuel's canoe for the twenty-mile paddle to Norway House where she was to stay with the Hudson's Bay factor's family for the night. The wedding was scheduled for the next day, Saturday, June 22, 1895. Despite the remote location – or perhaps because of it – Anna's wedding lacked none of the traditional trappings. She wore her full-length satin wedding dress, carried a bouquet of northern wild flowers, and cut an elaborately decorated wedding cake, contributed by the cook on the *Red River*.

It was not until the Thursday of the next week that the couple had packed their supplies for the nine-day canoe trip to

Nelson House some 200 miles further north over river, lake, rapids, and portages. The trip was difficult and strenuous, and often a heavy sea made the canoe roll and pitch at terrifying angles. But, as her husband explained, the native guides "will not run risks, but when in the middle of a lake [a] heavy wind comes up they have to go on...but Anna seemed absolutely unafraid." Near the end of the journey, however, exhausted by the long portages, the suffocating heat, and the swarms of black flies, Anna began to show signs of fatigue. Once when a heavy rain storm forced the Indians to stop, she admitted to Samuel how much she had dreaded the thought of a third portage after trudging over two that day already. During the trip Samuel had time to tell his bride the natives' comments about her arrival, which was the cause of great excitement among them. "'Just think', some of the Indian women exclaimed to me in awe before I set out to get you," he told her, "'she is coming from her far away land and she will not only come but she will stay with us here in our land. It is truly wonderful! I wonder if she will love us?'" Finally, at dusk on the ninth day, they arrived and Anna saw a rough cabin and the church on a grassy knoll where they stood out in stark relief against an endless barren skyline. "The Indians voted to have the church as near the center of the settled people as possible," Samuel told her, adding that "the Hudson's Bay people and a number of Indians live two miles further on and a mile across the lake in a little settlement."

Conditions were even more primitive at Nelson House than Anna had been led to expect. She threw herself into her new life and was genuinely interested in the Indians and eager to win their affection. When the Hudson's Bay factor's wife told her that the Indian women would like to see her in her wedding dress, Anna agreed to wear it to church the first Sunday. "Never had these native women seen anything so wonderful, and they looked upon both dress and wearer with something almost akin to reverence," her husband wrote. "At the close of the morning service, I had Mrs. Gaudin stand within the rail where they all came to shake hands, many also kissing her cheek. I was inclined to interfere when some attempted to go through it the second time. Others complained against these extras, saying 'You have already kissed her once'."

Soon, Anna began to receive requests for her medical services. Her husband remembered one of the first calls that came even before their chairs had arrived.

Anna was sitting on a low stool reading when a tall Indian in bare feet stood noiselessly before her. Startled for a moment she finally gathered by his signs that she was urgently needed. Following her strange visitor, she found a young man lying on the ground in an unconscious state. Strong coffee soon restored him and she then discovered that his chief trouble was a lack of nourishing food.

Before leaving, Anna made sure the Indian was fed and from then on she saw that he received supplies from the mission.

Anna started to learn Cree and soon was able to communicate satisfactorily with the Indians who came for help. According to Samuel, "calls from the sick began to pour in as soon as the people learned that the lady of the mission was a skillful doctor nurse." Anna's role as doctor-nurse, for which she received no financial remuneration or official recognition, was strictly voluntary. Missionaries' wives were generally expected to help out in the mission and were often called upon to nurse the sick, even though most had no proper training. In the 1860's, for example, Elizabeth McDougall, wife of one of the first Methodist missionaries in the North, used to hold the religious services during her husband's long absences visiting his area, and acted on occasion as peacemaker when the Indians became restless. Another missionary's wife, whose husband served in the same area, recalls that she was expected to look after visitors at the mission – washing, cooking, and cleaning for them, not to mention feeding them out of her own family's limited food rations. For this she received not a cent. Although Anna had few white guests – only four in one year – she too faced the problem of stretching her husband's meagre salary to buy enough medicine, bandages, and food for her Indian patients.

She was kept busy running the house and later raising her children as well as acting as doctor and nurse. She taught the Indian women who stayed at the mission from time to time how to cook, wash floors properly, make beds, and change the linen. This help allowed her to go out on calls at any time of day or night without worrying about her family's welfare. Word soon spread about Anna's willingness to go on any call, however inconvenient the time or however hazardous the journey. Old Indians in the area still remember the familiar sight of Anna carrying her bag following a silent guide through the dense woods to help an Indian in some remote settlement.

Anna never knew what to expect when an Indian came to her. In her thirty-nine years in the North, she treated everything from broken bones, accidents, and abcesses to various diseases. Samuel Gaudin was more explicit about his wife's cases:

> One of Mrs. Gaudin's many shorter trips of some twenty-five miles was taken to relieve a woman who had accidentally broken a needle in her hand and this was causing her so much pain that she got but little sleep. With the assistance of her native driver Mrs. Gaudin put the woman under an anaesthetic and by a little cutting of the hand the needle was removed, the hand bound up and the woman was soon sound asleep.

On another occasion Anna treated an Indian who had been badly hurt while carrying a heavy log from the woods to his canoe.

> This log along its extent had great sharp points left from the old fallen off branches. As he came down on the smooth slanting rock he slipped and fell. The sharp points tore his forehead across and then to the roots of hair and back cutting the top of his head. We happened to be away...but as soon as it was known that Mrs. Gaudin was home, a Royal

Canadian policeman brought the injured man over to the Mission for her attention. As it was already well on toward night Mrs. Gaudin had to operate by lamplight. He was first put under an anaesthetic. The hair on the top of his head was closely cut and the wound there was found to be not deep so that cleansing and sticking was sufficient but the one on his forehead was deep and long and turned at right angles joining the cut on his head. This required many stitches which were all cleverly done.

Whatever the problem, one thing remained constant – the unsanitary conditions. Usually, Anna found her patients lying in filth and squalor in a teepee crowded with children and vermin-ridden dogs. The living conditions of most Indians were so appalling she had to sterilize her instruments before setting out from the mission. She also set up a small cot in her own cabin where she could nurse the worst cases in more hygienic conditions.

Since some of Anna's calls came from areas as far as fifty miles away, she was often away from home. As a result, Samuel learned early in their marriage to do his share of the housekeeping. Because a man simply did not help with such traditionally female tasks as the washing or minding the children, some people thought the Gaudins' domestic arrangements odd. A fellow missionary recalls coming into the mission house and finding Samuel standing stirring the clothes on the stove with one hand and holding the Bible in the other. At that time people considered it just as strange for a woman to tackle such masculine chores as hanging doors and cleaning chimneys or fixing canoes – jobs that Anna attended to when necessary, since she was much more adept at it than her husband. As one minister put it, Samuel "was the type who knocked over the paint every time he painted a canoe. Once when the chimney caught fire both Sam and his son rushed to get the ladder at the same time only to end up pulling it apart." Many people thought Anna was rather too masculine. She always dressed in riding breeches when she went on the trail – something women did not do at the time, even in the North. Large-boned and approximately five feet eleven inches tall, Anna's height in itself contributed to this impression.

With so many things to learn and so many adjustments to make, Anna's first year of marriage passed quickly, leaving her little time to think about the approaching birth of her first child. Somewhat skeptical about the abilities of the Indian midwife whose lack of attention to basic hygiene frightened her, Anna prayed nightly that God would let her stay conscious during the birth so that she might direct the proceedings herself. Fortunately, her little girl arrived safely even though Anna finally passed out with the pain.

As the first white baby the Indians had ever seen, Irene roused a wave of curiosity and excitement which Anna was quick to exploit. None of the women had ever seen a baby being bathed, for example, so Anna invited them to watch Irene get her daily bath. "Look," she would say, "it doesn't hurt her, she's laughing." These hygiene lessons went on for several years as the Gaudin family continued to grow. Little Irene was soon joined by a sister, Ida, and a year after that by a brother, David.

As if her own babies weren't enough, Anna also found herself housing eight Indian children at the mission. The first of these adoptions occurred when she was brought a badly burned little Indian girl to nurse. The father, who had given up hope for the child and was anxious to return to his camp, told Anna, "You can keep her for your own if she recovers." Anna spent hours picking off layers of dead skin, dirt, and pine needles from the raw body, then applied soothing homemade salves. Because of her lack of supplies, Anna had soon learned to use local herbs and homemade medicines.

In time she became expert at concocting new medicines out of the supplies available. For instance, her balm of gilead made from buds of black poplar which she pounded while still sticky then simmered and strained through cheese cloth, added carbolic acid, and stored in cold cream jars, was very healing when put on wounds. Another medicine she used frequently for drawing out poisonous fluids from infected wounds was a castille soap she made from adding flour and water to soap chips.

In the case of the badly burned Indian girl, Anna's knowledge and care saved the child's life. Later Anna adopted her to prevent her natural parents from reclaiming her when she reached a marriageable age and could be of some use to them in their trading.

The other Indian children Anna had gathered under her roof were, for the most part, the result of casual unions between white men and Indian women. As they held no rightful place in the band, no one would assume responsibility for them. Anna, however, was not in a position to offer them a permanent home for Samuel's meagre salary was already strained by her habit of giving shelter to the sick she was nursing. The problem became critical when, in 1900, the Gaudins heard that they had been granted a year's furlough. Eventually they decided to take the adopted children as far as Brandon, Manitoba, where Anna arranged to put them in an Indian school. The plan seemed simple enough in theory but Anna had not reckoned on the mechanics of transporting eleven small children 400 miles by canoe, foot, and ship. To make matters worse, she herself became ill soon after they left Nelson House and had to make most of the journey on a stretcher.

When they reached Brandon, the school refused to take non-treaty Indian children, and Anna had to start searching for another school. She finally found one in Red Deer, Alberta – another 400 miles away. The Gaudins had no choice but to take their charges there. Anna agreed to keep their own three children with her and stop off at Moose Jaw to visit Sam's sister while Sam took the eight Indian children on to their school at Red Deer.

Soon after he left, their infant son became seriously ill. At first Anna thanked God it had happened when she was within reach of a doctor, but her optimism was short-lived for it soon became apparent that the doctor was as mystified and helpless as she. Through the long night, Anna helplessly watched the baby in his fight against death. By morning it was all over, and when Sam arrived back from Red Deer he found his son dead and Anna exhausted, grief-stricken, and bewildered at the irony of her loss. "It doesn't make sense that he should die here with a doctor to help when we have survived three years without one," she kept saying.

Anna and Sam travelled on to Quebec, where Anna slowly regained her strength and spirits. As she felt better, she grew tired of showing off her children and being treated like a celebrity and started to worry about the Cree she had left behind. She and Sam began accepting invitations to speak to church groups in Long Island and Montreal to tell people of the hardships suffered by the Indians in northern Manitoba. From these lectures, they collected enough money to buy medical supplies for the following winter.

By the time their leave came to an end, Anna was anxious to get back to work. Four years living in primitive, isolated conditions at Nelson House made her feel like an outsider in Quebec – a feeling that confirmed her belief that she had made the right decision in choosing life in the North. In 1901, the Gaudins returned to Nelson House to find that little had changed in their absence. Anna quickly slipped back into her busy routine, and once again the mission began filling up with sick Indians.

In the next few years, Anna gave birth to two more daughters, May and Josephine. Although welcome additions to the family, all the children combined with Anna's generosity towards the Indians she nursed once again put a strain on the family income. At the best of times rations where limited to the assortment of canned goods that came in by boat to the main mission at Norway House once a year and were transported by canoe the 200 miles to Nelson House. The Gaudins could supplement this with fish and vegetables, but they still usually ran short by June. Despite Sam's constant warnings, Anna continued to house and feed the sick and starving. "If a man stood at your door with his children and said piteously, 'For myself I am not afraid to die but will you not care for my starving children?' what could one do but share what one had with them?'' Anna would ask. She could not stand by watching starving, ragged Indians streaming into the settlement after a poor hunting season, pulling their large-eyed, sickly children on sleds. As a frequent visitor to their camps, she knew the grim details of their struggle with hunger. First, they killed all their dogs to save food and then stripped the bark off trees, boiled it and ate the sickly looking, putty-like mess.

By the end of the winter the Gaudins' meals had become almost as monotonous as the Indians' for their daily diet usually consisted of a stew-pot of fish and a handful of oatmeal. Sometimes Anna used precious bits of candle wax to fry the fish in an attempt to make a change. For white men living in the North in those years, the monotony of the food was a common complaint. Often they had to make their meal of one item such as fish which was usually served without salt and was followed by tea without milk or sugar when the rations ran out. As one missionary in the North pointed out, these deprivations were hard to ignore:

> For years pemmican has been a staple dish on our table, yet I must confess I have very little relish for tallow and pounded meat. My wife says that it is better not to think of bread while we cannot have it as the thought might cause us impatience. I shall not controvert her opinion, but judging from my feelings at this minute, the sight of a four pound loaf would produce in my poor heart the liveliest gratitude.

There was always great excitement among northerners when new supplies came in. Anna used to work on the list for a long time before Sam went out to the Church Conference in early summer. He would bring back crates of fresh fruit and meat to tide the family over the summer, then Anna would go to Winnipeg late in August when she took the children to school and order supplies for the winter. The Gaudins' difficulties with supplies were compounded by the fact that when a shipment arrived at Norway House, the Indians would pack their canoes with the crates that balanced best, regardless of what they contained. Their daughter, Esther, remembers one such incident:

> Often, we would open a box of curtain material when we were in desperate need of food. And on another occasion during a famine at the end of the winter Dad trekked two hundred miles to Norway House to bring back a box of supplies addressed to us. When we opened it we were sick to find it was filled with boots for the left foot only. The carton with boots for the right foot never did arrive.

Frustrating as this was, the Gaudins learned to accept such mix-ups as part of life in the North:

> Living so far from civilization taught us to be resourceful. In fact, one of Mother's favourite sayings to us was 'Necessity is the mother of invention' and this seemed to be true in our family. Dad built an ice-house to enable us to store the moose he shot and mother learned from the Indians how to cook wild birds, meat, and fish in many different ways to vary the taste. She used to dry moose meat and pound it into bits then cook it up with fat and flour so it seemed very much like hamburger. Later, when we moved to Cross Lake, Dad brought home a cow from one of his trips outside so we had fresh milk from then on. Even getting enough water took time in winter for Dad had to chop a hole through the ice on the lake and then carry it up in bucketfuls to the house. We kept a rain barrel outside but that water always turned brown.

In 1906, Samuel got word that he had been moved to Cross Lake Mission, about seventy miles away. It was with profound sadness that the Gaudins prepared to leave Nelson House. As Sam wrote later, "fifteen years of labor in eleven of which Mrs. Gaudin had shared, and where five of our children had been born, had endeared to us both place and people." Anna was disturbed that no nurse would be replacing her for she knew how much the Indians needed and depended on medical aid.

When they arrived at Cross Lake Mission, the Gaudins found a bleak, unwelcome looking parsonage.

We found the parsonage to be in great need of repair which meant very much labor before it could be made comfortable for the winter. The wind made its way freely through many places in the outer walls. The clapboarding had to be removed and three thicknesses of tarpaper put on as we went on with fresh boarding. Both gables were taken out and straightened. New and large windows were put in downstairs...partitions were torn down and others erected to make a good-sized medicine room which was Mrs. Gaudin's special domain. Throughout the house all the furnishing work was largely done by Mrs. Gaudin's hands. Before being papered the walls were covered with gray cotton pasted on. Then dining room, hall and study were completed with painted burlap topped with an oak finish. We then made a warm, comfortable home and by no means devoid of beauty.

Despite these renovations Anna found it hard to conceal her dislike for the new mission, and the hardships of that winter did not help to endear the place to her. Early in the winter, her third daughter, May, woke up with a sore throat and fever that soon developed into diphtheria. One of Anna's first thoughts was to find a refuge for her other children outside the infected house. There was little she could do for her daughter except soothe her and pray for her recovery as she had done less than three years before with her son. Again it was to no avail, and her daughter, only five years old, died later the same night.

Christmas 1906 passed with little celebration, and in the New Year Anna became increasingly worried about the risk of infection. "She was convinced that the wretched house still harboured the ghosts of the dreadful diseases," her husband wrote to his superiors. As it turned out, Anna's fears were justified. In mid-June, just eleven days after Nelson, the sixth of Anna's seven children was born, Ida, Anna's second child, contracted diphtheria despite all the precautions the Gaudins had taken to save the other children from infection. Fifteen days later nine-year-old Ida was dead. The loss plunged Anna into a deep depression that soon affected her health. Her milk dried up but the wife of the Hudson's Bay factor, who had just had a baby herself, volunteered to nurse the Gaudins' baby.

Sam, himself quite shaken by the series of disasters, was worried by the obvious effects their recent loss had had on Anna. In his letters to the mission board he pointed out how much his wife had suffered: "Our baby was only eleven days old when Mrs. Gaudin had to be over Ida almost day and night. I need not say how hard this double affliction has been on her." In subsequent letters written during that summer, Sam noted repeatedly that his wife was "far from well" and that "the extreme anxiety has told against her very much." Both Gaudins began to question whether they were justified in subjecting their children to life in the North. As Sam commented in the same letter to the mission, "We hardly know what to do and we can hardly understand how the disease has originated and how it has been so confined to [our family]. We have suffered much already and we do not know but there may be more ahead." Thinking that a change might help Anna's condition, Sam took her and the children to Toronto and Winnipeg for the summer. But when they returned, Anna soon succumbed again to her long-standing hatred for the Cross Lake Mission.

By this time it had grown into an obsession which was not helped by daily confrontations with medicine men who did their best to frustrate her efforts at nursing the Indians. Frequently she would find the entrance to a patient's teepee blocked by a stern medicine man who would follow her if she took the sick person to the mission for treatment. Sam tells the story of one Indian who came to Anna for help and was put in a tent near the church. "Suddenly she heard a very loud voice as though a quarrel was going on in the tent. She ran around [and as] she entered the tent found...Keewatin, a noted conjurer and father of the sick man, had his son's breast bared and from it he was exorcising an evil spirit that he claimed was the cause of his son's illness. 'See,' he said as Mrs. Gaudin entered the tent, 'It's right there,' and he pointed to a special spot on his son's chest." When the boy did not recover under the influence of his magic, the old medicine man concluded that "it was too near the church for the best results, and he moved [him] away from such baneful influences." The boy died within a few months. Incidents like this continued, regardless of Anna's attempts to use more scientific cures on the sick. In another case, a young boy at Cross Lake suddenly suffered a severe hemorrhage:

> I happened to be near and the poor father came over to me half crazed with grief about the condition of his boy. I hastily crossed the river and rushed over for Mrs. Gaudin, and we were soon over to the house but to our suprise we were locked out. The secret of this was that Indian medicine was in operation and if we were allowed in we might spoil the whole affair. Mrs. Gaudin felt very badly but there was nothing we could do except return home. The poor boy did not long survive.

This was not the only problem confronting the Gaudins at Cross Lake. Three years after their arrival, Sam wrote a rather discouraging letter to his superiors: "Christian life is by no means very much in evidence. Apathy and indifference to spiritual things is characteristic of the people in general...We have tried to reach the people by the regular services, by visiting them [and by] helping them in material things...[but] we have not seen such results as we longed for in our work." In these circumstances, Anna seemed unable to regain her previous vitality and strength. Even after the birth of her seventh and last child, Esther, she still brooded on the deaths of her children. For every child born, one seemed to die, and Anna grew nervous every time one of her children caught even the slightest cold. When Josephine complained of a sore throat one night, Anna and Sam expected the worst. In his letter to the mission board dated December 8, 1909, Sam's dignified but matter-of-fact account contained more than a hint of resignation: "On Monday night at 6 o'clock we lost our little Josephine by croup after but one day of serious illness. We laid her away this afternoon between little Ida and May." Jo was the fourth child the Gaudins had lost; now only three remained of the seven Anna had borne.

Fortunately, Anna's schedule kept her so busy that she had little time to brood over her personal losses. In addition to her work at the Cross Lake Reserve, she made regular visits to outlying areas, covering distances anywhere from twenty to 120 miles. Her husband recalls that on one occasion she was on the trail eleven days as she went among the far distant hunting camps during an epidemic of la grippe. Sometimes she slept in her carriole so that she would be ready to give attention to the sick when she arrived at another camp.

For a long time after Josephine's death, Anna had suffered from a lump in her throat which she attributed to her sorrow. However, when she took time one day to look inside her throat, she found a small tumour. Aware of the potential dangers but reluctant to make the long trip to Winnipeg, Anna decided to operate on herself and send the tumour into Winnipeg for a biopsy. Anna said nothing, but waited until Sunday when the family would be in church. Then, with the help of an Indian woman who held the mirrors, she cut deeply around the growth to be sure she got the entire tumour. When it was out, she placed it in a bottle, sewed herself up and then proceeded to tend to her assistant who had fallen to the floor in a faint. Only when her husband smelled the disinfectant did she confess her secret. After a long wait, the results of the biopsy reached Cross Lake showing that the growth was benign.

As their three surviving children grew up, they left Cross Lake for schools in the south. Sam Gaudin's reaction when Irene, their oldest child, went to Flesherton to high school, was mixed: "It was hard on us...to have her so far away, but we thus arranged that she might have opportunities for education which she could not have if we left her with us in the far North." However, the arrangement proved frustrating in times of illness. One day in the middle of winter, the Gaudins received word that Irene was very ill. "We at once began preparation to make the eight-day journey by dog team over the lake...By nightfall we had gone forty miles...and the next day arrived at Norway House post office and received letters with good news of Irene's recovery." Sam had to return home immediately but Anna waited two weeks for the next mail to be certain everything was indeed all right before heading back.

Hard as it was for Sam and Anna to be separated from their children, it seemed to be equally hard on the children who all said they were often homesick and lonely during the years they had to spend at school. Today, Esther admits, "When I was a teenager, I even felt I was deprived – deprived of the parents and home that other children enjoyed year round and deprived of the life I had grown accustomed to in the North."

In the twenty years the Gaudins spent at Cross Lake they saw the power of the medicine man dwindle in face of the Indians' growing trust of the white man's treatments. In 1919, however, there was a terrible outbreak of influenza among the Indians of the Cross Lake area. "It swept through communities like wild fire," recalled Sam. Anna, of course, was out over the reserve ministering to the sick and dying, night and day, with little rest or sleep. Her meals were often eaten standing as she prepared medicine or food for another visit. She sometimes carried wood at night from wherever she could find it to start a fire in some cold house where all were down sick. Anna had foreseen the ravages of the sickness and sent off an s.o.s. for government aid. Then she learned that the 'flu epidemic had hit the rest of the world, and every community was too busy fighting its own battle for survival to worry about the Indians. One of the worst aspects of the epidemic was that the Indians were particularly vulnerable to this white man's disease, and in some of the distant camps whole families were almost wiped out. In one such camp Sam reported that there were "thirty-one persons among whom were a number of good hunters, but when the epidemic had spent itself less than half survived and not one hunter remained."

During this crisis, Anna received word that she had been appointed Matron of Cross Lake Reserve, a distinction that gave her the authority to obtain the supplies she needed. Added to this honour went a salary – her first in twenty-three years of service in the North. But even the church's recognition of her work could not bring Anna out of her depression or revive her exhausted strength. For a long time she could do nothing. "I can't see anyone today," she would tell Sam day after day and retire to her room where she would simply close her eyes and rest.

In 1922, a short time after the 'flu epidemic, Sam was appointed to Norway House, the largest and most civilized mission in the area. Situated at the hub of various outlying missions, it had a school, a doctor, and a hospital. Anna recognized Sam's appointment as a long-overdue promotion, but nonetheless she felt a wrench at leaving the people among whom they had worked for twenty years. Her worries were the same as those she had had on leaving Nelson House after eleven years: Would another nurse replace her? Would the Indians get the medical help they needed so badly? Would the newcomers appreciate the Indians' habits and fears?

At Norway House, Anna confronted a new set of problems. She was no longer the only medical expert in the area, as she had been at Sam's other two posts. At Nelson House and Cross Lake, she had grown accustomed to handling difficult cases that had really required a doctor's attention. She had given anaesthetics, sewed up wounds, performed minor operations, treated serious illnesses, and delivered babies. Also, because of the shortage of medical supplies, she had learned to make use of and had come to rely on the medicinal powers of various herbs and barks. Now, at fifty-seven, she suddenly found herself in a setting where her homemade remedies were questioned and her skills restricted to specific functions.

Anna often clashed with the doctor, who was relatively new in the area. He tended to go by the book and looked askance at many of Anna's methods. Consequently, she only went out on calls when Indians asked for her and in this way she was able to continue with her homemade remedies. Even years later Anna used one of her unorthodox remedies on an Indian in an outlying area who had suffered for six months from a dreadful itchiness caused by a rash that had covered his entire body. Sam described how the doctor had given instructions for the man to be taken by his sons to the Norway House Hospital.

> [Felix] refused to go and finally came with his wife to Mrs. Gaudin's little hospital at the Mission. His condition received close study and when we finally decided on his trouble the only remedy available was corn starch poultices. With the assistance of a nurse who was visiting friends, thick poultices of the starch were put on him from his head to his feet, his wife also helping in the operation, all being kept in place by bandages. This remained on him about a day. The poor man was delighted with the relief this remedy brought as for the first time in six months he slept soundly throughout the night and his body was clean and clear from the old disease so that not even an itchy feeling remained.

But despite such dramatic results, Sam realized that everyone was not as happy as the patient.

Anna and Samuel stayed eight years at Norway House. In July 1930 they returned to Cross Lake, which had become their "favourite place." Four years later they were ready to retire and moved to Transcona, Winnipeg, to live with their daughter Esther Ross and her family. Anna died four years later in August 1940 at the age of seventy-five.

Left: Martha Black (1866-1957). Right: Peggy Shand (1851-1943). Above: The Chilkoot Pass, which they both crossed in the 1890's.

CHAPTER THREE

Gold Fever:
The Lure of the North

Many of the women who widened the range of experiences available to other women were unconscious of the part they played in the struggle for women's rights. Some revolted a-gainst traditional boundaries not so much from a desire for broader intellectual horizons as from a lust for adventure. They turned their backs on comfortable lives and joined the Gold Rush of 1898, making the tough and dangerous journey by steamer and then trekking inland over hazardous mountain trails to the Canadian territory of the Yukon.

All types of people from all parts of the world seemed to have caught this latest outbreak of gold fever. Barbers, streetcar operators, newsmen, busboys, dancers, musicians, doctors, waiters, clerks, and businessmen, as well as pimps, card sharks, gamblers, hawkers, and saloon impressarios quit their jobs, sold their possessions, and headed north aboard one of the leaky, sea-worn, and overcrowded steamers that had been hastily salvaged from the dry-docks. During the late fall of '97 and the early spring of '98 alone, some 40,000 people dragged themselves and their supplies and equipment, weighing up to 1,000 pounds per outfit, over the Chilkoot Pass. Of these, only a very few were women.

Generally speaking, the women who did go north were of two kinds: the dancehall girls, and the adventurous daughters of middle- or upper-class families. The former, who usually hid their identity under such names as Diamond-Tooth Gertie, Nellie the Pig, Ping Pon, Diamond Lil, and Klondike Kate, were an integral part of the wild frontier society. As the ditty puts it:

> The Miners came in '49
> The whores in '51
> They rolled upon the barroom floor
> Then came their Native Son.

These girls did not have to worry about their respectability, and needed only the courage to face the hazards of the trip and the fortitude to withstand the primitive conditions of the North. Like many of the men, they dreamed of making their fortune.

Kitty Rockwell, better known as "Klondike Kate," believed that if she could reach the gold fields, she could earn enough in a short time to put herself and her mother on easy street for the rest of their lives. For most, however, there was a great gap between their dreams and the reality that awaited them in Dawson where, although they did well enough financially, many of them led wretched lives. Usually they were attached to pimps, gamblers, and thieves, lived in small rooms above the saloons, and catered to rough men who thought nothing of paying fifteen dollars for a bottle of champagne to be drunk in the company of a pretty girl. Some of these girls managed to marry one of their wealthy, free-spending miners, settle down in respectability, and forget about their former lives. "I sometimes think I must be the only dance-hall girl left from the Yukon, for I am the only one who admits the past," Klondike Kate once remarked. Kate had become a celebrity in the Yukon and could afford not to be ashamed of her past, but other dancehall girls, even after they married, continued to be ostracized by respectable women.

While the dancehall women added colour and contributed to the reckless excitement of life in Dawson during its golden era, there was another, less notorious type of women in the North. They had been lured north not so much by stories of gold as by the attraction of its vast empty spaces, an attraction that continued to draw devotees long after the Gold Rush ended. These women were among the adventurers who looked upon the northlands as the last North American frontier, "that meeting point of savagery and civilization where man could pit his resources against nature in an atmosphere of relative freedom."

For women who were frustrated by their role in Victorian society, life on the edge of civilization symbolized freedom and the opportunity to use their talents. "I could not shake off the lure of the Klondike...that vast, rugged country...I felt its mysterious drawing power," wrote Martha Black in 1899. Like a few other middle-class women with courage and a strong desire for adventure, she had disregarded the opposition of her family, turned her back on her sheltered Victorian existence, and headed north to the Yukon, where survival depended on personal courage, resourcefulness, and strength. Women who went to the Yukon needed these qualities even at the outset to overcome their families' almost certain opposition to their unconventional and dangerous journey. In the public imagination, the Yukon was a land of rough, dirty miners and loose, bawdy women living together in a climate of easy money. So pervasive was this view, in fact, that a decade after the Rush, when twenty-nine-year-old Laura Berton headed north to teach in Dawson, her father was appalled at the prospect. Despite his Quaker upbringing and career as a freelance journalist, he still thought of Dawson as a decaying, decadent city long past its golden days of fame and wealth with dirty, unshaven miners sitting idly as life passed them by.

Although such women as Laura Berton and Martha Black had rarely had to exert themselves physically before, many of them rose to the challenge of their new environment and seemed to thrive on it. Martha Black found life in the Yukon "a vigorous challenge." She had to contend with 60-below temperatures, the long, dark winters, and the tormenting armies of flies in summer. To cope with life in an isolated cabin a mile outside Dawson, she had to shed many of the Victorian ideas on which she had been raised, such as the belief that all strange men were just waiting to pounce on unattended women. "There were times of tough sledding," she admitted about those days when she had to support herself and her family, but she had no regrets. "I liked the life...I had faith in myself...that this tide in my affairs would lead me on to fortune."

Laura Berton had times of "tough sledding" too, but she came to sympathize with the lot of women in the Yukon. Many marriages broke up because the wives, unable to adjust to the harsh, lonely life in a land they saw as hostile and threatening, left for the "outside." Like Mrs. Berton, many of these women had been brought up on fears of woods and men. Here they were surrounded by miles of isolated, dark, unknown bushland, and often left alone for days when their husbands had to make trips for supplies or work. Women also suffered from the very real fear of dying in childbirth, a fear Laura herself faced eight years after her marriage. Two of her friends in Dawson had died giving birth, and few people in Dawson expected Laura, by then forty-two years old, to survive the ordeal. But she surprised them all by producing a healthy son (Pierre Berton), followed by a daughter the next year.

In this land where so many men and women had died, or simply given up and gone "outside," some of the most sheltered women, such as Laura Berton, Martha Black, and Peggy Shand, not only survived but grew to love the land and the way of life it demanded. Given the opportunity, these women all showed an amazing capacity to adapt and cope in difficult conditions, and none of them ever seriously considered returning to her former life, even in times of trouble. And although none of these women discovered gold, the lure of the North was the fulfilment and meaning they found in their rugged environment.

Peggy Shand

When Peggy Shand's husband burst into their small California ranch house one night in July 1897, he brought news that was to change their lives. Peggy listened with mounting excitement as Davy raved on about "nuggets as big as potatoes," including one that weighed twenty-one pounds and was said to be worth $5,700. "I tell you gir-rul, if I had money for my expenses and your passage back...to Scotland, I'd be on my way tomorrow...We haven't the money anyway so don't let's fuss about it." Still, he could not stop dreaming about the Gold Rush, nor were his circumstances likely to make him forget the possibility of making a fortune in the Yukon.

Now, less than ten years after he had written Peggy, his childhood sweetheart in Scotland, that he was ready to settle down and provide her with a proper home, he was facing financial problems. Soon after they had settled in San Francisco poor health, caused by years of travelling around the world in search of excitement and money, had finally forced Davy to settle down and exchange his well-paying business activities in the city for a farming life. For the Shands, by now in their mid-forties and with no knowledge of farming, the ranch was proving a financial disaster. Like thousands of stampeders in 1897 and 1898, Davy burned with a gold fever that made him fix his hopes for a better life on getting to the Klondike, whatever the cost. He continued to pour out stories and make plans until Peggy, too, was affected by his obsession. "I am going if you do," she told her husband, and that was that. "I hadn't the least idea how a woman, a sheltered woman as I had always been, would fare in this wild, cold country, and Davy tried to explain it to me." She won out in the end, however; he agreed to let her come as long as she promised not to complain when the going got rough.

From the beginning the trip demanded total commitment.

They had to sell their home and all their personal possessions to raise the money for their passage north and for the special equipment for the rugged life in the Yukon. Although Peggy had made the suggestion, she had not realized how difficult it would be to part with all the things she had brought with her from Scotland when she came over to marry Davy less than ten years before. "Keep with you only the clothes you wear and a few personal things you can carry yourself," Davy told her. At last Peggy began to appreciate the rigours that lay ahead: "I grasped the fact gradually that we would make most of the trip on foot and somehow pack hundreds of pounds of equipment along with us...that we would have to hurry before winter would be closing in and there would be no shelter much of the time."

Peggy did not have much time to worry in the excitement and activity of getting ready. While they awaited passage north from San Francisco, she had herself fitted for a dark blue, English storm serge travelling suit with fashionable balloon sleeves. Davy took complete charge of organizing their supplies and arranging for a passage on a sea-worthy boat. "We'll not risk our lives on any of those old tubs that might go to pieces as soon as we get out of the harbour," he had insisted after looking at some of the old, rusty freighters that had been pushed into service to handle the sudden rush of passengers. And so it wasn't until late August, 1897, that the Shands managed to get a passage on a ship Davy had approved.

After considerable discussion with other passengers about various routes inland from Alaska, Davy opted for the Dyea Trail. This route entailed landing at Dyea, a tiny tent settlement at an inlet on the coast, and hiking in over the Chilkoot Pass to Lake Lindeman, a distance of some thirty-six miles. From there, they would sail down the Yukon to Dawson, arriving before winter closed in, some time in October. The plan sounded straight-forward enough since they would reach Dyea on September 7, 1897 and would have over a month to make the trip.

Their first day on the trail was hard enough to dampen

their enthusiasm. Even though Peggy went on horseback, she was exhausted and discouraged, for after hours of travelling they had gone only a few miles. To make matters worse, Peggy's horse had stumbled crossing a stream, throwing her into the ice-cold water. Fortunately, the big balloon sleeves of her jacket filled with air and helped to keep her afloat until the men pulled her out "shaking with cold and fright." But the heavy woollens she had chosen for the northern climate refused to dry by the fire they built and were still damp when Peggy and Davy resumed their journey.

The journey became progressively more difficult. The trail that began at Dyea wound down the canyon of the Dyea River but then began to rise towards Sheep Camp at the base of the mountain. This part was a gruelling trek for unconditioned fortune-hunters weighed down by packs of eighty to a hundred pounds. The Shands, who were already approaching middle-age, were ill-prepared for such a physically exhausting journey. Davy's doctor had told them that Davy would never be strong again after an illness he had caught in South America a few years before, and Peggy's nerves were not up to the grim warnings she received daily from men who were horrified to see a woman on such a dangerous trail. As an Irishman put it bluntly:

> [Watch] going up that steep bluff just ahead – so many accidents happen right there. People have heavy packs on their backs and the trail runs along so close to the edge of that stony cliff. Just one misstep and you get overbalanced. You can slide off the trail mighty easy and go down into this deep water. This place don't seem to have any bottom, it's a kind of whirlpool. Many's the one who's gone down and not come up. I've seen it.

Davy himself was no more encouraging: "You go down and we can never rescue you," he told his wife. Nonetheless they reached Sheep Camp at the base of the mountain and, with the help of some Indians, cached their packs alongside the tons of supplies deposited by other weary travellers. Ahead lay the infamous Chilkoot Pass known as "the worst trail this side of hell." It began at Sheep Camp and wound four treacherous miles up to the Summit, which was 3,500 feet above sea level and marked the boundary between Canada and Alaska. By the time the Shands reached Sheep Camp, the pass ahead was covered with snow, adding yet another danger to their journey. But there was no time to hesitate, and they joined the stream of travellers hurrying over the trail to reach Lake Lindeman before freeze up. "My pack did not seem so heavy when I started," Peggy recalled.

> I struggled along, climbing, climbing, and it grew heavier until I felt I had the world on my back. The straps cut and galled my shoulders. The weight and the climb put a strain on my muscles. Underfoot was rough going; my feet slid over the rocks. At times I had to crawl, using my hands and feet in a constant effort, lifting and pulling upward...It was hard to breathe. My heart pounded in my ears with sickening nausea. A tottering weakness shook my knees...People filed by us in a continuous stream...it made me think of an army of ants.

Suddenly she heard Davy scream out, "Look Peg! It's an avalanche." Turning, she saw a wall of water and ice that crashed down the mountainside sweeping everything before it. Helpless, they watched men running for their lives, tearing the packs from their shoulders to run faster. Peggy stared in awe: "The packs fell in the terrifying, moving, slipping avalanche and were quickly carried out of sight. And then it was all over. The mountainside had been swept clean."

There was nothing to do but go on as time was running out rapidly. In 1897 the freight services that would later transport stampeders' supplies to Dawson had not been started, nor could the Shands afford to pay Indians to pack in their supplies. Like many others, they had to carry in everything themselves, bit by bit, storing it, as was the practice, in caches along the route. Peggy feared their things would be stolen until one man explained that it wouldn't be healthy for a man to be caught rifling a cache."I saw two fellows try that trick," he said. "There weren't any Mounties to attend to them, but they formed a Trail Committee which is made up of men along the trail. They held court and gave the thieves a trial. Some of the men said 'shoot em' but others said 'no.' One of the thieves took his own gun and shot himself...The other was bound to a tree and lashed, and a sign put on him, 'I am a thief.' A few lessons like that and a fellow knows men mean business."

Convinced their packs would be safe, the Shands piled their things together, clearly labelled them, and set off back the trail for more. Peggy remembered with horror those weeks spent packing back and forth from one cache to another.

> We grew so tired and weary we would lie down on a pile of driftwood and fall fast asleep while people streamed by us. Men bent double under the weight of their packs. There were Indian packers, dogs trotting swiftly and easily along the trail, women dressed in overalls, with caps on their heads looking almost like men, carrying all they could manage. No one paid any attention to us, sitting beside the trail. Many others just as weary were resting when they could.

By far the worst of all this was that Davy had not figured on how time-consuming this procedure would be. His mistake led to the first of a series of disasters that completely disrupted the Shands' future plans. As the couple hurried to beat the winter, the Mounted Police sent orders that no more small boats could be used on lakes and rivers because of the running ice. The Shands were trapped in Sheep Camp for the winter. This was disappointing enough, but they soon learned that their entire outfit, which they had cached at Crater Lake after carrying it so laboriously across the Chilkoot Pass, had been swept away in a snowslide.

"Now what will we do?" Davy asked helplessly. "There's no hope of getting anything until spring. All we have left are a few things cached here at Sheep Camp. We have no money to live on, because things cost so much, nor have we enough money to go back."

Then a man offered Peggy fifteen dollars a day to make biscuits and pies in his hotel, but Davy balked. "I will not allow my wife to work as long as I am able to care for her," he told Peggy. Obediently, she turned down the job but she never forgave Davy for spoiling her chance to make money. As Davy would not let her accept a paying job, Peggy arranged to cook in exchange for free room and board at the mill where Davy had got a job.

In the spring, with enough money to start anew, they left their jobs and travelled back to Dyea. By this time, freight services to Lake Lindeman had been established and they did not have to repeat the ordeal of the previous fall and pack in a second set of supplies and equipment over the Chilkoot Pass. But before they could start for Dawson, Davy was caught on the trail in the last snow storm of the year. As the hard, driving snow hit his face, he felt sharp pains shoot through his eyes. Snowblindness. He recalled stories of men driven mad by the pain of it. When at last he staggered into camp at Lake Lindeman where Peggy was awaiting him to sail downstream to Dawson, he was in agony. Peggy tried to make him comfortable but nothing relieved his pain. Week after week it went on and Peggy watched helplessly. April passed and he did not improve. Then two weeks of May, and still no change. Each day Peggy went to see if their second outfit, containing food, medicine and tobacco for Davy, had arrived by freight from Dyea but returned empty handed.

Finally Peggy decided to hike the twenty-four miles from Lake Lindeman back over the Chilkoot Pass to Dyea to find out about the missing outfit and get medicine for Davy's eyes. She had hired a man to cook and look after her husband, and then set out in the middle of the night in the hope that the top ice, which had melted on the lakes and rivers during the day, would be refrozen. When she reached the shoreline she saw that six feet of water separated the shore and the solid mass of ice on the lake that bore the trail. If she took the path along the shoreline, she would run the risk of meeting bears. As she stood trying to decide which route was less dangerous, a stranger appeared. He, too, stopped to gaze indecisively at the ice.

"I'll take a chance on the ice if it's at all possible," he said. "You know about the bears, don't you? They are just waking up from winter and I don't fancy meeting one now." This remark was all Peggy needed to opt for the lake for, after one winter in the North, she could recall any one of a dozen stories of people killed by hungry bears.

"You stay ten feet back of me and if I don't go in, it'll be all right," the stranger said cheerfully. "But if the ice gives, turn back and run like hell!" With this warning, he turned and was off, leaving Peggy to follow as best she could. By the time he reached the far shore, Peggy had fallen so far behind he merely waved and left her to make it on her own through the waist-deep water near the land.

Soaking wet, she was hurrying along the trail to keep warm when she saw a man near the Summit. Dressed in fine new clothes with a heavy watch-chain swinging from his plaid vest and an overcoat over his arm, he seemed ominously out of place on the deserted trail.

"Hello, there?" he greeted her. "You're a right good-looking gal. When we get you dressed up, some of the fellows will fall for you, all right." Peggy was terrified. If she tried to run, he would realize that she was frightened, and besides, she might not be able to run fast enough to escape. At that moment she spied some people coming along the trail. When they stopped to greet her unpleasant assailant Peggy saw her chance, and in a flash she was away, running until she reached Sheep Camp, where she spent the night under the motherly eye of the innkeeper.

The next morning Peggy was off early to Dyea where she learned that the outfit they had bought had been lost in transit. When the company agreed to pay part of its value, Peggy immediately accepted the offer, not wanting to waste time haggling for more while Davy lay waiting at Lake Lindeman. She hurried to buy medicine, tobacco, and a few other supplies and set out for home without further delay. Spurred on by the worry that the man she had paid to stay with Davy might have left him helpless, Peggy walked day and night until she reached home.

With the proper medication Davy's condition began to improve. At first he had only partial sight in one eye, but at least he could take care of himself. Although he was forced to postpone his prospecting plans, he was well enough that summer to take a job operating an engine at a saw mill on Sullivan Island at the mouth of the White River, one hundred miles from Dawson. With one winter's experience as a cook, Peggy easily arranged to cook for the work crew in exchange for her keep. After the mill closed at the end of the summer, the Shands formed a partnership with three other men to run a roadhouse opposite the mouth of the White River. The men built the stockade roadhouse, leaving Peggy to do the cooking, cleaning, and bed-making for as many as twenty guests a night. Even before the place was half finished, a steady stream of travellers bringing merchandise over the Yukon ice trail to Dawson stopped to beg for shelter and, no matter how full the roadhouse, Peggy took them in.

All winter I cooked over the little stove. We had room for only six at a time at the small table...and each traveller [had to] wait his turn...My experience in cooking for men at the mill stood me in good stead and I was able to cook and manage very well...Night or day the door was likely to fly open and a half-frozen traveller, hungry as a wolf, would dash in. On such occasions I always climbed out [of the bunk by the door] to cook a good meal even though I might have just climbed in to get a little rest.

When winter was over and the men dissolved their partnership to go their separate ways, they split the profits four ways, taking it for granted that a woman did not expect payment for doing household chores. "I felt hurt and angry, but did not say a word," Peggy confessed later, but blamed herself. "Let this be a lesson to you the next time – make arrangements before you go into a thing — men never find it necessary to count a woman's work!" When she was offered a job as cook at the lumber mill the following winter, Peggy agreed only after her employer had signed a firm contract.

The summer of 1899 brought a new series of disasters for the Shands. Davy had taken the roadhouse as his part of the profits and had used it to store the couple's new outfit and all their winter clothing while he and Peggy tried their hand for the first time at prospecting. Then, during the summer, the place burned to the ground. Penniless and in debt after their unsuccessful prospecting venture, the Shands faced their third winter in the Yukon once again destitute and discouraged. Fortunately, they had both been promised jobs at the lumber mill for the winter. But even this gave them no financial security as the owner gambled away all his possessions, leaving Davy and the rest of the work crew to race into Dawson to beat the creditors to their wages. While they were away, a band of thirty-odd Indians raided the camp where Peggy had been left alone. "They took all the tea and coffee and when they had cooked and eaten, they wanted to trade with me showing me a few ragged pelts. All the time they jabbered in their own language. Their beady black eyes that were never still were watching me...'When man come?' asked one, but I was too smart to tell them that Davy would not be back for days." By this time they had squatted around in a circle and begun to drum with their hands and feet. Then one young squaw leapt into the middle of the circle and began to dance. A young man soon joined her and together they danced in close to Peggy, pulling her by the hair and gesturing with their knives. Then they shoved a gun in her face. At first she was too scared to move or cry out. But then she caught on. "They were having fun at my expense, and it made me angry. Waiting till the girl was in front of me, I pushed her in the stomach with all my angry strength, making her fall backward. The Indians howled and laughed...and I took the center of the circle myself." Tossing her head and humming the music, Peggy danced the Highland fling. The Indians were first surprised, then pleased.

After they left, taking most of her supplies, Peggy waited anxiously for her husband's return. When days passed without word, Peggy feared the worst. Then Davy staggered into camp so weak from pneumonia that he had had to abandon all the supplies he had bought in Dawson. Near starvation herself, she tried to summon her failing strength to nurse a delirious man hovering on the brink of death. "I wondered if I, too, would go mad, raving mad, like Davy." Although she ate next to nothing herself to conserve food, she managed to cut down trees and split them into logs to heat the cabin. Her time inside was spent trying to get some food into the near-skeleton on the bed. She applied countless hot plasters to his chest, but he grew weaker as the high fever took its toll and the cough tore his lungs.

At night, Peggy could hear the hungry wolves outside the cabin, jumping at the windows and scraping the door. She had begun to give up hope when she heard the voice of an old friend outside. Jack MacDonald had thought the Shands might be in trouble after the mill closed down and had trekked out to the camp with provisions. Together he and Peggy pulled Davy through the crisis.

Jack stayed on for a time, helping them to get started again. Only when he was preparing to return to his prospecting did he confess how lonely his life was and how much he would miss the gay and happy Peggy. "Somehow, I had never thought of Jack romantically," Peggy said. They had met first on their journey down the Yukon River in the summer of 1898 when Davy was recovering from his snowblindness, and the three of them had become friends.

The Shands had now spent three winters in the Yukon but they finally were ahead of their problems. They accepted the reality of Davy's poor health, discarded their impossible schemes of prospecting, borrowed some money, and bought a small roadhouse on Stewart Island, at the busy junction of the Stewart and Yukon rivers. Although the place was crude, it had potential. Made of logs, it contained seven rooms downstairs, and five rooms and thirteen-bed bunk-room upstairs, all furnished entirely in "sourdough" or homemade furniture. Over the years the Shands made improvements as their finances allowed and brought in furniture from the outside. The business prospered from the beginning, partly because Peggy, who had developed considerable confidence in herself and her business sense in the past three years, decided to run the place herself instead of leaving it to her impractical husband. But the key to their success lay in their strategic location; anyone travelling to or from the lead and silver mines had to pass the Shands' place. Often people would have a two- or three-day wait for a boat at the roadhouse, and needless to say, Peggy was constantly busy. Each day she baked bread, cakes, pies, and puddings, often working till late at night.

For the next twenty-nine years, Peggy did all the cooking, cleaning, bed-making, and dish-washing for her guests. During the short summer seasons she used to plant, weed, and tend a vegetable garden as well. Peggy certainly had not expected life in the Yukon to be so physically exhausting, but their financial difficulties and frequent mishaps coupled with her husband's impracticality meant she had no choice but to work.

Peggy's cheerful approach to life made the roadhouse a favourite place for thousands of visitors and soon earned her the name of "Little Mother of the North." She always treated her guests with warmth, sympathy, and understanding, and when strangers were brought in suffering from frozen feet or hands, Peggy nursed them. One old sourdough remembered the comfort she brought him: "I was new to the country, sick and in bad shape, without enough blankets in my bedroll...She doctored me...and did all she could...I'll never forget her." Knowing that such men would be returning to isolated stakeouts, Peggy always urged the sick to stay on at her hotel until they were fully recovered, whether or not they could afford it.

Yet when the occasion demanded, Peggy could be just as tough as some of the guests she encountered from time to time. Once an Englishman and his servant arrived at the roadhouse. When the servant informed Peggy that his master required a separate table as he did not wish to eat with "these people," she listened in amazement. "No, not here," came the prompt reply to the astonished servant, who retired to inform his master. In time, driven downstairs by hunger, His Lordship condescended to sit at the large table with the other guests. His valet, however, persisted in hovering around, trying to anticipate his master's every whim. Exasperated, Peggy told him to sit down. "Your master will get enough to eat and if he doesn't it is quite his own fault," she said. Later Peggy explained to His Lordship that he would have difficulty getting along with people in the North because he was violating a motto she and other northerners cherished: "One man was as good as another. It was the real man that counted, not the money and fine clothes."

All the time Peggy remained on tiny Stewart Island, she never felt cooped up or restless.

> In those years, I met more interesting people than if I had crossed the continent. The cry of "gold" had brought men from every land! Bishops and high church officials, governors and judges, military officers, professors, scientists, explorers, and miners, titled Englishmen, millionaires, writers, and poor men with their picks and shovels. I had the opportunity of meeting these world travelers in a way few had.

Just by talking with such a variety of people she had received a broader education than she could ever have had in a ladies' school or college.

Peggy also blossomed intellectually in this busy and cosmopolitan atmosphere. She found her knowledge expanding and her curiosity aroused by subjects she had never had time to read about in her youth when the Bible was all she was allowed in her spare time on Sundays. "I felt I had read the Bible enough," Peggy claimed and so in slack periods at the roadhouse she read the histories of Europe, America, South America, and anything else she could get from the Mounties, who kept her supplied with books.

Although Peggy enjoyed her years at the roadhouse, at times the life was hard. On four separate occasions, the place was completely flooded when the ice went out. The first time, they were just beginning to feel more settled and secure. The hotel was doing well and they had brought in furniture from the outside, and even built a greenhouse with special glass Davy had ordered.

The worst disaster occurred in 1918 when the roadhouse burned to the ground just before Christmas, leaving both the Shands badly burned and almost destitute. Davy never completely recovered and he was bedridden all the winter of 1919 as his strength slowly ebbed away. Peggy spared no expense and ordered medicines from outside. Although she still had to run the roadhouse, she nursed Davy until he died in August 1920.

Once again, circumstances prevented Peggy from brooding over her loss. In going over Davy's effects, she discovered that he had accumulated a number of debts in connection with his many schemes to make them rich. Pride forced Peggy to work to pay them off. As the loneliness and financial problems took their toll on her health, she was forced to move to Dawson for the winter. To her surprise, Dr. Chappell, whom she had known for many years, took her to his own home until she regained her strength. By the time of the break-up, the doctor had persuaded Peggy to come and live with his family permanently. She set off on the first boat to sell her hotel and make arrangements to live in the doctor's home.

Once again Peggy arrived at the island to find the roadhouse in shambles. This time Peggy welcomed the work as it kept her from thinking. Dr. Chappell stopped off at the roadhouse as he went past one day to tell Peggy that he would be back to get her later in the summer. But only a few days after he left in his boat, Peggy was surprised to find his spaniel barking at her door. Fearing the worst, she hurried to the police barracks and, after a brief search, the doctor's boat was found upside down, but his body was never recovered. Peggy was shattered. Another long winter at the roadhouse lay ahead and, although she would be busy, she was no longer young and the work tired her.

More than a year after Davy's death, Peggy received a letter from her old friend Jack MacDonald asking her to marry him. "I have a nice farm and a good house all ready for you," he wrote, and promised to be on the first boat after break-up. Peggy was stunned. She wrote back a warm, friendly letter asking him to come on a visit to Stewart but was non-committal on the question of his proposal: "It would do us both good to talk over old times, but I could not promise to marry."

However uncommitted she had been in her reply, throughout the long winter she spent alone, Peggy found herself thinking about her old friend's proposal and as the break-up time approached, she grew restless and excited. The day the first boat arrived Peggy was nervous. "I put on a new dress and even a touch of powder," she admitted, then went to watch for Jack as the passengers disembarked. Even when the last one had filed by her, it never occurred to Peggy that he would not be on board. "He might be talking to the captain," she thought, refusing to believe that he hadn't come. But she had to hurry back to the roadhouse to serve lunch to the hungry new arrivals. Then she saw someone laying a letter on the sideboard. It was from Peace River but it wasn't Jack's handwriting. She waited until dinner was over before she tore open the letter with trembling fingers and read:

> I am grieved to tell you that my brother Jack died just a week ago from pneumonia. His death was very sudden. He had been working hard to have things in perfect order on his farm. He was bringing back a wife, he told us. He did not say who she was, but I knew you were the only woman he loved. I hasten to send you this sad message, as no doubt you will wonder at his not arriving on the first boat.

It was signed simply "Jack's brother." Peggy felt lonelier than ever: "No more could happen...All ties were cut now – my family, Davy, the kind doctor, Jack – no one left." For the first time in her life she gave in to self-pity: "What would become of me?" she wondered. "I realized I could not run the hotel any longer. I was sick and miserable [and] had no one to turn to."

Then "like a dream," as Peggy put it, a letter arrived from her husband's nephew, who had been searching for Davy and Peggy for years. Relatives in Scotland had at last sent him the address of the roadhouse. Peggy answered at once and soon received a reply asking her to come and make her home with them in southern California. Although it was a wrench to break her ties with the North after more than thirty years, she decided to accept the offer: "I wanted to be with my husband's relatives, and since I had a chance to sell the roadhouse to people on the Island, I could afford to make the move."

Peggy lived with her nephew and his wife for fourteen years in their large San Diego home, where she died in 1943 at the age of ninety-two. Even though she was approaching her eighties when she moved there, her nephew's wife wrote that her "unusual magnetism attracted new friends wherever she went." Fittingly, in California as in the Yukon, she is remembered for the compassion that had prompted lonely people in the Yukon to tell her their troubles. "She would pat your arm and say 'Everything will be all right, lass' and you knew by her touch that she understood your problem." In the Yukon the oldtimers never forgot her. When her niece visited the Yukon they told her that "It was not what she said, nor anything she did, but just the great understanding within her heart which radiated as a warmth, something lonely men could feel." It's small wonder she was known as "Little Mother of the North."

Martha Black

Martha Louise Black's most significant moment came in 1935 when at the age of seventy she ran as a Conservative candidate in the federal election. Her win at the polls proved that enough people in her Yukon riding thought a woman was the "best man" for the job, even though Canadian voters had elected a woman to Parliament only once before when Agnes Macphail won a seat in the House of Commons in 1921. Mrs. Black's victory was a step forward for Canadian women in more ways than one; she had broken into traditionally male precincts, the House of Commons and the Yukon constituency. This accomplishment would have been no small distinction for a woman at any time, but in the face of the Liberal landslide of 1935, it was exceptional.

Martha Black could not have chosen a worse time to run for Parliament. The Depression was crippling the country, and the public was disenchanted with the government. As the wife of George Black, the Conservative Member of Parliament for the Yukon since 1921, Martha was bound to be associated with the Conservative Party and with R.B. Bennett, leader of the Conservatives, who had led the country since 1920. Even though she ran as an independent Conservative, she was still linked to Bennett's image of big business, in a country that was now looking elsewhere for leadership.

Canadians were surprised, therefore, that the seat in the Yukon remained Conservative, but even more so when they learned that a woman had won it. In fact, few people, including newsmen, had paid much attention to the campaign waged by the woman in the Yukon. When Mrs. Black's son, Lyman, called up the *Winnipeg Free Press* on election night to find out how his mother had fared, his question was passed around the newsroom until someone finally came up with, "Oh, that other dame." Obviously, Martha Black had not been expected to win.

Generally speaking, the paper's attitude was indicative of the rather skeptical views most Canadians held at the time on women in politics. "What can this damned old woman do for us in Ottawa?" women in the Yukon asked each other. Others were bitter enough to accuse her of running "a sob-sister campaign." Martha Black, waging her campaign against this sort of prejudice, hurled back tough replies. "What if I did...I would have sobbed louder if necessary," she told her critics bluntly. "You'll be lucky when you reach my age if you have my sturdy legs, my good stomach, my strong heart and what I like to call my headpiece."

Her campaign had been very different from any other in Canada. She had travelled across the 200,000 square miles of the riding by foot, jeep, row-boat, and horse and wagon in order to call on its 8,000-odd constituents, the majority of whom were men. "I once walked several miles to visit three voters, one of whom had declared himself 'agin' me." Later she heard that she had got all three votes. There had been times, however, when the trials of electioneering made Martha wonder why she, a woman of seventy, had ever agreed to run. On those days she would tell herself "You should have been spending...the sunset of life knitting, resting, reading, or pursuing your best loved hobby, the gathering and study of wild flowers."

Her full schedule had left little time to worry about what her life would be like if she did win. In fact, she started to consider the responsibilities of her new role only when reporters began questioning her about it. "What did you do to reach this high point in your career?" they kept asking her, only to learn that she had had no political ambitions. "Career?" she used to reply, "I never had a career...never wanted one." But after she had taken her seat in Parliament among men who had devoted their lives to getting elected, Martha became aware of the irony of her victory.

Near me is my colleague, Miss Agnes McPhail (sic), who, at the age of thirty-two, was the first woman to be elected to the Canadian House of Commons, and who had been returned term after term. I know that she has deliberately sacrificed love, marriage and a home, that she might give herself entirely to the parliamentary advancement of Canadian women...Across from me is the Right Honourable, the Prime Minister, W.L. Mackenzie King...I know that he has given a lifetime of service to reach this eminent position...he is seeing the enactment of legislation and the establishment of principles for which he has worked all his adult years.

On her right was the leader of the Opposition, R.B. Bennett, who had "worked faithfully and unswervingly toward a fixed ambition to which he has given a sincere and ardent devotion, even to the detriment of his health." For the first time in years Martha felt inadequate. The only thing she had given up was her position as wife of an M.P. with which she had been "eminently satisfied." Martha Black had, in fact, been pushed into politics by chance. As she was the first to admit, she was no more than a political "pinch-hitter" for George Black, who had been the speaker of the House of Commons and Member of Parliament for the Yukon since 1921. When he had suffered a serious mental breakdown and was unable to run in the election campaign of 1935, several of his constituents, aware of his wife's enormous abilities and "the half-jocular claim that in [the] Yukon there are but two political parties – the Liberals and the Blacks," suggested that she run in his place. At first she thought the idea preposterous. But the more she pondered her future, the more Martha felt she must take this opportunity, just as in the past she had taken advantage of any opportunity that might make life exciting, full, and rewarding. Besides, as she said, there was the material angle of earning a living to consider. George Black's illness had, of course, stopped their income and Martha knew only too well what this meant to them financially. So she accepted the nomination and plunged into the strenuous campaign.

When she won, she faced the larger problem of proving to the country that she, a woman, could be as effective and intelligent a member of Parliament as any man. Martha had no illusions about her obligation to Canadian women; she knew that as the second woman to be elected to the House of Commons, any mistakes on her part would inevitably influence the chances of other women. This responsibility weighed heavily on Martha, who felt suddenly intimidated despite her success in her various former occupations.

Hansard leaves little doubt that she took her responsibilities seriously; she participated actively in parliamentary debates in all areas that concerned her constituents or her personal prejudices as a woman, a mother, an imperialist, and a Conservative. Her views were predictable for someone of her age, sex, and background. She felt obliged, for instance, to speak for Canadian women. On the day after Parliament opened in 1936, she rose in the House and asked that the sympathy of Canadian women be extended to Her Majesty, the Queen, on the death of her husband, King George V.

Martha was equally outspoken when defending the "mother country," cadet training, and the Union Jack. As might be expected from a lifelong member of the Imperial Order of the Daughters of the Empire, Martha's arguments reflected her staunch belief in imperialism. She was fiercely opposed to Canada having a separate flag because, as she told Parliament, "when [foreigners] came to [Canada] they came under the protection of the Union Jack, knowing what the Union Jack stands for on land and sea in Australia, in New Zealand, in India, in Canada itself."

Martha Black's concern for her job was more remarkable in view of the personal tragedy which clouded her private life during the high point of her public life. She had just got over the emotional upset caused by her husband's nervous breakdown when she received word that her youngest son, Lyman, had been killed in a car crash. Martha and Lyman's wife, Aimée, who acted as her secretary, had been waiting in Ottawa for him to arrive from Belleville for the weekend when they received the news. "We were stunned beyond words," Martha wrote in her diary, on February 27, 1937 the day of the fatal crash. But Martha's feeling of responsibility to her constituents helped to make her keep up with her busy schedule. Only her diary testifies to the strain she underwent. On March 15, 1937, she wrote, "At the House – carried on as usual. Some days – feel fresh and able to go on – on others it is with great difficulty that I can whip myself up to take any interest in people or my work."

Within six months of Lyman's death, her eldest son, Warren, and her only brother, George, both died unexpectedly, and again she took refuge in work and in writing her autobiography, *My Seventy Years*, which was published in November 1938. The next year, she wrote a book on Yukon wild flowers, published in 1940. The same year her husband reclaimed his seat in Parliament causing at least one reporter to write, "After watching his wife's performance [George] had a substitute ...whom he will find hard...to replace in the esteem of political friend and foe alike."

But while Martha had many friends in Parliament who often praised her for her "kind and genuine" words, she had no influence – nor could hope to have any influence – in the predominantly Liberal government. Her constituents had mixed beliefs in Martha Black's abilities as their representative. "The Honourable Mrs. Black was always thinking of us," claimed one woman in Whitehorse; while another stated that the "old gal just kept the seat warm for her husband." The few contemporary Conservative M.P.'s still alive today recall that she was "a nice old lady" with "exciting stories of her life in the Yukon," but no one can recall anything she accomplished as a politician. But Martha never really saw herself as a politician, and confessed that "given the choice between being mother of a large family [or a politician] I would choose the former." Basically, she preferred the role of politician's wife to M.P. for she had never had much taste for statistics nor many of the other issues that she had had to study as an M.P. In fact, considered in light of her past life, Martha Black's position as Canada's second woman M.P. seems ironic indeed. Unlike women like Agnes Macphail who were driven by strong political desire, Martha Black had never felt the need to fight for women's rights. As she readily confessed, chance and an innate zest for adventure were the underlying forces responsible for her unusual and varied life. It was these factors that caused her to make her initial break with convention when she left her role as Chicago society wife and mother behind in the 1890's and adopted an exciting new lifestyle in the Yukon.

Martha's first marriage to Will Purdy in 1887 had begun with a whirlwind honeymoon on her father-in-law's private railway car. After they settled in a suburban home in Walden, ten miles outside Chicago, Martha found that on Will's salary of a thousand dollars a year she could afford a maid and had time to enjoy her new-found freedom as a married woman. "My first thrill of freedom came with my marriage when, at last, unchaperoned, I could go to the Vienna Bakery, a place with a naughty reputation," she recalled, adding how embarrassed she had been on her first visit there when one of her uncles had walked in with a blonde.

In less than a year, Martha's first child, Warren, was born and was soon followed by a second son, Donald. For the next few years Martha was engrossed in the duties of motherhood, and it was only in retrospect that she understood that her concern for and interest in her two small sons slowly undermined her marriage:

This period in a woman's life is the most difficult to weather. It is then she realizes that the first glamour of romance has gone; that she must settle down in earnest to the business of living. She must figure out the adjusting of the ever-increasing living expenses to an income which, with most, does not increase in proportion to the mounting costs of raising a family.

When gold fever hit Chicago in 1897, it immediately infected Martha's first husband. Will Purdy. Will was bored
with his routine paymaster's job with the railway and anxious
for a change, as was his friend, Eli Gage, son of the president of
the First National Bank. Together, they made plans to join the
Gold Rush and, backed by their wealthy fathers, formed the
Purdy-Gage Company and bought two ocean-going tugs, one
steamer, and two sailing vessels.

As she listened to their plans, Martha longed to join the trip
north. She had nothing to keep her at home; her husband was
going and her parents had offered to take her two sons for the
summer.

At the time, all she wanted was some excitement. The only
problem was how to convince her husband to take her to the
Yukon with him. She was in luck. An employee of the Rock
Island Railway by the name of Lambert got word that an uncle
of his died in the Klondike and willed his family a million
dollars in gold dust, and some very rich properties. The young
man showed a copy of the will to Martha's father-in-law, who
suggested that Martha could act as the Lamberts' agent to
collect the legacy. Lambert not only agreed, but signed a contract to pay Martha fifty per cent of the gold dust (a half million dollars) if she retrieved his inheritance. "This was the real
factor in the final decision concerning my going," said Martha.
"To me it was a quest that had all the allures of a 'Treasure
Island' or 'Aladdin's Lamp'."

The trip north began when Martha and Will said good-bye
to their children and set off for Seattle. However, as soon as
they arrived in Seattle, Will was called to San Francisco on
business where, according to Martha, he heard such terrible
stories of the hardships of the trail that he changed his mind
about going to the Klondike. He wrote to Martha, asking if she
would consider going instead to the Sandwich Islands where he
had heard great fortunes were being made. "After ten years of
marriage, how little he knew me," she said. "Go to the Sandwich Islands? With my Klondike ticket bought, my passage

booked, my vision of a million dollars in gold dust?" Meanwhile, the Gages had left for Alaska where Eli got sick making them abandon all interest in the Yukon. "Miserable and heartbroken as I was this was my opportunity to seek and claim my fortune...I could not turn back." Realizing that she had had enough of her marriage and her undependable husband, she wrote to Will saying that she had made up her mind to go to the Klondike as originally planned, and that she never wanted to hear from or see him again. Martha got her wish and never did see Will Purdy again: they were divorced quietly in 1899, and her husband died in 1900 in Honolulu.

Although she had made the decision, Martha still had to persuade her brother to let her go without her husband to protect her. At first he refused to take any responsibility for her and even threatened to send for her father, but eventually he gave in.

For Martha Black, nothing would ever match the trip to Dawson in the summer of 1896, a trip which, from the beginning, turned out to be a series of nightmares. To start with, Martha had no idea of the confusion caused by the thousands of frantic fortune hunters heading north at the same time. Although some prospectors had succeeded in reaching Dawson by the fall of 1897, only months after news of the discovery had reached the outside world, the bulk of the gold-seekers were not prepared for the journey until the summer of 1898. Martha had never met people like those suffering from gold fever. Driven by visions of fortunes awaiting them in the Yukon, they agreed to any price, any inconvenience, any injustice, in return for a passage north. If anyone complained of being cheated, he found his place taken by another. When Martha boarded the small coastal steamer on which she had booked and paid $120 for a private stateroom, she found to her surprise that it was already occupied. The double lower berth had been allotted to a tin-horn gambler and his female companion, the middle to Martha and the upper to "Birdie" who was to become one of the most notorious characters of the Klondike. Angry and embarrassed, Martha and her brother protested to the captain and purser, but were told they could take it or leave it. And take it she did. Martha had no intention of giving up the trip whatever the inconveniences or embarrassments caused by this invasion of her privacy. As the sheltered, wealthy, convent-educated daughter of a successful Chicago businessman, at thirty-one Martha had considerable adjustments to make. At first, she was so upset that she used to weep at the strange sleeping arrangements, but by the end of the trip, she had made friends with her cabin-mates. "Every morning the gambler brought me coffee, and I heard his bedfellow tell him, 'You see that her toast is thin, you know she has a delikat stummick'. Birdie, too, often gave me an orange or apple from her supplies." Martha, however, could not get used to the appalling conditions elsewhere on the sea-worn steamer. It was dirty and loaded to the gunwales with passengers, animals, and freight. Men slept on the floor of the saloon and in every corner. The captain was seldom, if ever, sober, and there were wild parties, poker and black jack games and drinking night and day.

The conditions did not improve much when she disembarked at Dyea, the tiny tent settlement from which Martha and her brother planned to continue their journey by foot over the Chilkoot Pass, then by river to Dawson. As Martha stood beside their outfit on the sandy shore and looked at the bleak cluster of tents strung out along the beach, wedged between the icy black water and the towering mountains, she began to realize the enormity of her undertaking. The forty-two-mile hike ahead involved walking, or, more accurately, scrambling, over the slippery, narrow trail that wound along canyons, through rivers, and across mountains from Dyea to Lake Bennett. As the Shands had done the previous fall, they went first to Sheep Camp at the foot of the Pass, then up to the Summit, down to Lake Lindeman, round the shores of the lake, past the rapids and finally to the little village of Bennett.

The first day out their destination was Sheep Camp at the foot of the Chilkoot Pass. The gruelling hike was bad enough in itself but some of the sights along the way had made it worse. "On every side," Martha recalled, "were mute evidences that we were indeed on a trail of heartbreaks and dead hopes. [There were] scores of dead horses that had slipped and fallen down the mountain-side, and caches of miners' outfits." At one point they looked into a deserted cabin and saw a ruined outfit lying moulding on the floor. "Home of two brothers who died from exposure last winter," they were told. When, at last, exhausted and disillusioned they reached Sheep Camp, they were greeted by the sight of a huge pile of snow, ice, rocks, and debris from a snowslide that had recently killed more than thirty people.

The ordeal of crossing the Chilkoot Pass remained stamped on Martha Black's memory for the rest of her life. She looked on it as a symbol of her ability to surmount any obstacle. Every time she retold the story, she relived the horror of those hours when she had scrabbled, slid, stumbled, and finally dragged herself over the treacherous trail. On July 12, 1898, she took her place in the continous line of pushing humans and straining animals. Unlike most people in the line, however, Martha and her friends could afford to hire packers to carry their several tons of supplies – clothing, bedding, and food. Even so, they found it heavy going. To add to her difficulties, Martha's movements were restricted by her fashionable clothes which she had carefully selected for the trip – the Jaeger combinations, merino stockings, high boots of Russian leather with elk-hide soles, a natty straw sailor hat and the last word in an "outing" costume of the late nineties. Always interested in fashion, Martha used to boast later that her brown corduroy skirt was five yards around at the bottom and a "shockingly immodest length" because it showed her ankles. At the time, however, she realized how foolish and unsuitable her clothes were. She soon shed the sealskin jacket but could only curse the hot, high buckram collar, the tight heavily boned corsets, and the full bloomers which she had to hitch up with every step. After they reached the Summit, Martha relaxed, thinking the trip down would be easier. But the last two miles into Lindeman were the worst of the whole trip. Finally she gave up and George picked up his exhausted sister and carried her into the settlement. The worst was over. They now faced only a short hike around the lake to Bennett, then a two week boat trip down the Yukon and they would be in Dawson – and within easy reach of the Lambert inheritance – or so Martha thought.

She had not expected there would be any difficulty in claiming the Lambert inheritance. "I had only to go to the world-famed goldfields, lay before the Canadian authorities proof that I was the family's agent, and collect the gold." Later she wondered how she could have been taken in as she was, or persuaded to go on such a wild goose chase. She certainly was not prepared for anything like the unruly, muddy, crazy town of Dawson in 1898, where, she soon found, corruption brought on by easy money was rampant. She had to bribe officials to procure the documents she thought she needed, only to find that they were of no help. Finally, with her money almost gone she gave up, convinced that the whole affair was either a huge hoax or an unfathomable mystery. All she had discovered was that Lambert actually had existed; that he had been a prospector in the far corners of the North for many years; that he had last been heard of in Juneau, Alaska; and that the will was in his handwriting. Martha had little choice but to tell the Lamberts the disappointing news. By this time, however, the Lamberts suspected that Martha herself had absconded with their fortune. They dispatched a lawyer to track her down and retrieve their inheritance. Only after he could produce no new information would they accept that their case would remain, as Martha put it, "one of the unsolved mysteries of the North."

By the time Martha abandoned her quest, she had little time left to get out before winter closed in. As she prepared to join the stream of disenchanted people departing daily from the land they had struggled so hard to reach only months before, she learned to her dismay that she was pregnant – by the man she was determined to divorce. She realized she could never walk back over the Pass, but after a summer of bribing officials, she had very little money left to pay for proper medical care which, like most services in the Yukon, was only available at an outrageous price. Her brother was of very little help in coping with the situation for which he partially blamed himself because he had consented to her coming North to begin with. Like most of their group, he half-expected Martha to die. In fact, when one of their friends went outside that fall, he told relatives that Martha looked so ill that she would not survive.

Martha surprised them all. "My old fighting spirit came to the rescue," she said later. "I suppose it is the pioneer spirit, not to be overwhelmed by trouble, but to arise and go forth to meet it." Realizing she would have to have the baby in Dawson and cope as best she could by herself, Martha turned her attention to preparing for her baby, cutting up her dresses and sewing them into little clothes during the long dark winter months.

The baby arrived ahead of time. The men had already left the one-room cabin for the day when Martha's pains began so strongly that it was impossible for her to walk the mile into Dawson for help. While she was still able, she set out all the things she might need, frantically trying to recall details from the births of her other two children in the Chicago hospital where, as a socially prominent woman, she had had the best medical care. Martha was lucky. It was an easy birth and the child, a boy, was strong and healthy.

Lyman's birth was only the first problem Martha had to face that winter in Dawson, and she quickly learned that the more exciting life she had wanted had its drawbacks. Lonely, poor, cold, and hungry, she spent six months in the tiny cabin entirely without butter, sugar, or milk. Prices of even basic necessities were exorbitant in the Yukon; flour was a dollar a pound, meat two dollars a pound, eggs three dollars a dozen, oranges, apples and onions a dollar and a half each – when they could be had. Cow's milk was sixteen dollars a gallon. Martha remembered how she had longed for some fruit or vegetables. Instead, she gulped down her unpalatable cornmeal mush with prunes and tea.

In spite of the difficulties, when her father came to Dawson the next summer to persuade her to return home to attend to her affairs, Martha was reluctant to go. But with scarcely any money and no means of earning a living in Dawson, she had little option. On her return to Chicago she found life there as unbearably stifling as ever. Finally, in June 1900, word reached her that some earlier investments had paid off. Martha packed her bags and, with her father's financial backing to supplement her own profits, headed north again. This time, she took her eldest son with her, but once again counted on her parents to look after the two younger children. They agreed to follow her the next year and bring machinery to start a saw and quartz mill.

In the interim, Martha set about building a new life for herself. She started by forming a claim-working partnership with two men at a mining camp near Dawson. Her job included doing cooking for the entire party. It was not a life of leisure as most of the provisions were in dried form and it took time and ingenuity to concoct even palatable meals out of the unappetizing stock of dried goods. That year she also began writing a journal that she was to keep for the rest of her life.

In 1901 Martha's parents arrived as planned and her father set up two mills on the Klondike River about a mile from Dawson. When he left he made his daughter manager of the mills, an arrangement that irritated some of the staff who declared they weren't "goin' to be run by a skirt."

The fall and winter passed uneventfully, but towards spring there was trouble with the mill hands. Although she paid the same wages and granted the same working conditions as other mills in the area, Martha sensed an undercurrent of resentment among her work crews. But when she criticized the foreman, he not only would not listen to her but incited the entire crew to resign unless she withdrew her remarks. Martha fired both crews rather than give in to threats. "It was the height of the busy season. Another raft of logs was due immediately. Orders were coming in beyond my fondest hopes, and here we were closed down." But she refused to change her decision. News of her firm stand won her considerable praise from men in the community, and within three days she had signed on a complete new crew and was ready to start up again.

The mills prospered under Martha's management and provided her with a substantial income. And her love of gaiety and pretty clothes soon made her one of the most popular women in Dawson. She attended dinner parties, card parties, skating parties, family picnics, dances, and gala balls, and was squired about by dozens of suitors who were lonely for a "touch of the homelife." Over the years, she received at least one marriage proposal a fortnight: "If I missed I thought I was falling off and getting old," she said, although she confessed that Yukon women did not have much competition. All the women of Dawson, including Martha, went to endless trouble to dress in the latest fashions, especially for the gala balls, which were the highlight of the town's social season. For these occasions, Martha splurged on some sensational gown from Dawson's most expensive dress shop, Mme Auger's, which was stocked with Paris originals costing up to $500 a piece.

Although Martha admitted she loved pretty things, her attention to clothes was not meant to impress Dawson's narrow-minded and self-righteous society ladies whose insistence on "what was proper" brought out the rebel in her. On one occasion, these women barred the local dancehall girls from the new skating rink. Martha sided with the outcasts who, in the end, won their case. They were allowed to use the rink, but received an emphatic warning that "if any girl was caught smoking or using profane language in the ladies' dressing room, her ticket would be forfeited." Martha had come a long way since the days she had cried herself to sleep because she had to share her stateroom with a prostitute.

On another occasion, she helped a local madam keep the real nature of her boarding house secret from her mother who came to Dawson to visit.

"Why not rent one of my mill cabins...and I'll see that your mother has plenty to do over the week-end," she had suggested to the distraught madam.

Frequently, however, Martha's unconventional behaviour seemed more intended to shock than to help. Once she jolted prominent Dawsonites by inviting her washing woman's daughter "to pour" at a reception, an honour traditionally reserved for the wives of the town's most prominent citizens. Later she told her critics that she was the daughter of a "washerman" and could see nothing wrong with asking the daughter of a washerwoman to pour. She failed, of course, to mention that her "washerman" father owned a nation-wide chain of laundries.

Since coming to Dawson, Martha Black had built a new, busy, and happy life for herself. "I liked the life, the vigorous challenge of it, the work, the play of it," she recalled. "Except for my relatives, I was entirely out of touch with Chicago friends and associations...[but] my business brought me in touch with all kinds of people – good and bad." More importantly, Martha had a new sense of independence and achievement born of her success in her job and her popularity in Dawson. Her life seemed to lack for nothing, least of all a husband who could only interfere with her new-found independence. She could not help but be skeptical of marriage after her problems with the impractical Will Purdy and she had little inclination to settle down with any of her many suitors. Then, by chance, she met George Black when he gave her some legal advice on a problem at the mill. "I liked him at once," she recalled. "He was good-looking and clever...serious and a good companion, and as we talked, I learned he was interested in politics and had a sincere desire to serve the Yukon." She invited him home, and two weeks later he proposed. But despite her interest, Martha was still wary of marriage, and although they saw each other frequently, it was two years before they were married.

Martha's second marriage resulted in a considerable change in her life. Since she no longer needed to support herself and her children, she sold her interest in the mill and settled down to raise her family and enjoy her life-long interest in wild flowers. Not only did she soon become an expert in the field but won prizes for her collections and lectured on the art of preserving and mounting various flora. In 1909, she accepted a part-time job with the Canadian Pacific Railway preparing wild flower collections for their display cases in hotels. This offer came at an opportune moment since George Black's law practice had fallen off as the population of Dawson dwindled.

The Blacks decided to move to Vancouver where George was soon admitted to the British Columbia bar. In the meantime, Martha's work for the C.P.R. took her across the province collecting various flowers. While she was away she left her boys on a friend's ranch and her husband to his own devices. In this way, she spent most of two summers on what she later described as the happiest missions of her life.

In 1911 Martha had to put aside her interest in wild flowers and accept the demands of a new and busy life – that of Chatelaine of Government House, the Yukon. In an unexpected victory, Robert Laird Borden's Conservative government had defeated Wilfred Laurier's Liberals at the polls, and the following year, George Black was appointed Commissioner of the Yukon.

"Filled with joy at the opportunity to live again in the country we both loved so well, accompanied by Donald [her second son] and Lyman [her youngest son] we left for the North in March," Martha recorded in her journal. Her life ahead was to prove as controversial and active as her past ventures.

During the four years she presided as chatelaine of Government House, Martha spent much of her time fixing up the house. Her aim was to turn it into "a beautiful house of the people," and with this in mind she redecorated, expanded the greenhouse, built a root cellar, started a henhouse, and landscaped the grounds. The staff at Government House – cook, housemaid, butler, gardener, and assistant – who had watched the house fall into a state of disrepair over the years, were somewhat skeptical about Mrs. Black's ambitious improvement projects but they found it easier to go along with them than try to resist the strong-willed Chatelaine. However, when Martha was planning her first reception and gave orders for "a thousand sandwiches, forty cakes, twenty gallons of sherbet, and the same quantity of salads," the cook and butler's ill-concealed amusement showed what they thought of her. As it turned out, her estimate of the appetites of her Yukon friends was accurate.

The new chatelaine loved the social side of her role and entertained expertly and frequently during her husband's years in office. Her parties were always lively, and often controversial. At her first reception, she disregarded the traditional highly selective guest list for Government House functions and invited "all who wished to come, irrespective of social position." It was an attempt to give miners, prospectors, and the like – most of whom had never been inside Government House – the tribute she felt they deserved for opening up the Yukon. Needless to say, the bluebloods of Dawson were appalled. However, much as Martha Black defied convention, loved gaiety, and indulged in practical jokes, she was adamant about maintaining respect for the office her husband held. Old friends learned that they could not trick Martha into breaking her own rules. When a sourdough rang up asking, "May I come over tonight and bring the Missus?" she would ask him outright whether or not "the Missus" was his real wife. Often she would remark, "You have already introduced me to several wives and George and I owe a duty to the dignified office he holds."

George Black was happy with his job as Commissioner, but with the outbreak of the First World War, as more and more men from the Yukon signed up, he, too, felt it his duty to serve overseas. Martha, never one to be left behind, prepared to go overseas with him by taking the St. John's Ambulance course in first aid. But when, in the spring of 1915, George enlisted, she learned what a difficult business it was to untangle the yards of red tape which would permit a wife to go on a troopship with her husband. Martha made full use of all her contacts in government circles. She visited the Prime Minister, Sir Robert Borden, and Sir Douglas Hazen, Minister of Marine, in Ottawa, and General Bigger, Officer Commanding Transportation, at Halifax. Eventually, her efforts paid off. In early 1917 she left Canada, the only woman on board a ship carrying 2,000 troops.

Martha's war years were typically active and varied. She worked in the London headquarters of the Red Cross; she maintained a constant open house in her tiny London apartment where boys from the Yukon spent their leaves and enjoyed the home-cooked meals she concocted from their pooled rations; and she visited members of the Yukon Company in hospital, brightening their days with news from home. She was in a good position to do this for, by this time, she was the official correspondent for the *Dawson News* and the *White Horse Star*. For three and a half years, she "listened to shrieking sirens and saw the aeroplanes and those horrible zeppelins on fire and falling in flames, with many men jumping from them." And, like all soldiers' wives and mothers, Martha lived in constant fear for the lives of her husband and three boys. It was not until August 1918, however, that she received "one of those dreadful telegrams." *Sincerely regret to inform you...Captain George Black, Infantry, officially reported admitted to Stationary Hospital.* Despite her efforts to find out more, that was all she knew until a letter arrived a few days later from her husband making light of his "blighty," caused, he told her, "by a slam in the leg with a chunk of shrapnel."

After the Armistice, while her husband served with the Army of the Occupation, Martha Black was sent to France by the Overseas Club to visit soldiers' cemeteries and war-devastated villages to tend and lay wreaths on the graves. By the time Martha had finished her tour, her husband had ended his duties and together they returned to Canada where they settled in Vancouver. Shortly after their return, George decided to run as a member of Parliament for the Yukon. After his victory in 1921, they moved to Ottawa, and for the next fourteen years the Blacks wintered in the capital, summered in Dawson, and spent the intervening months travelling the 4,000 miles between the two.

Martha enjoyed her days as an M.P.'s wife. From the beginning, she regularly attended sittings in Parliament, little suspecting that the knowledge she was absorbing would prove invaluable during her own political career more than a decade later. She also entertained frequently, especially after her husband was appointed Speaker in 1930, a position that included organizing and presiding at many official government social functions.

This pleasant life ended abruptly in 1935 with George's mental breakdown and her own election to Parliament, but after her term in office Martha was only too glad to step down in favour of her husband. George was not only re-elected but held the seat until 1949 when he was defeated at last at the age of seventy-six. The Blacks decided to return to the Yukon, settling first in Dawson, then moving to Whitehorse when the capital was relocated there in 1953. George continued to practise law, and Martha, although by this time confined to the wheelchair where she was to spend the last seven years of her life, kept busy pursuing her interests in wild flowers, politics, and writing. She was in the process of updating her autobiography, to be called *My Ninety Years*, when she died in the fall of 1957.

Today, many of her papers have been salvaged and are stored in the Territorial Archives in Whitehorse – a legacy of the extraordinary life of a woman whose name had become inextricably linked with the Yukon during the fifty-nine years she had lived there.

Margaret "Ma" Murray (1888-   ).

CHAPTER FOUR

By-Lines

Economic circumstances played an important, though indirect, part in the fight for women's rights, since financial need was often the initial impetus that forced women to pursue a career. Finding themselves without money, women who had never contemplated a life outside the home found themselves joining the work force. Some found nothing but drudgery in their new jobs, but others discovered a more fulfilling, stimulating way of life. Kathleen Blake "Kit" Coleman was one of the latter. Had she not needed to support herself she might never have become a journalist and made a name for herself as one of the best in the business.

Born in Ireland in 1864, Kit left her husband and emigrated to Canada in 1884. Despite her youth and lack of money and training, she was determined to start a new life. On the advice of a friend, she wrote some articles for *Saturday Night* and, as a result, was offered the job as women's editor at *The Mail and Empire* in Toronto. It was not long before Kit began opening up new horizons to her women readers by running such controversial articles as "Is Marriage a Success?" and "A Comparison of English, American and Canadian Girls." She aimed to expose women to the fact that there was a world beyond that cluttered by cookbooks and fashion plates. Equally important as her writing in helping to change women's view of their role in society, was the example she set by her own unconventional lifestyle.

In 1892 she travelled alone to London to write a series on the places Dickens had made famous. In 1893, she was sent as special correspondent to report on the Chicago World Fair, and in 1897, she was sent to cover Queen Victoria's Diamond Jubilee. Then, in 1898, against the advice of the paper and her friends, she set out on her own to cover the Spanish-American War.

When she arrived in Washington, armed with her credentials, she still had to persuade Russell Alger, American Secretary for War, that a woman could act as a war correspondent. His permission was finally granted, but her difficulties were only begun. The next six weeks were passed in Port Tampa, Florida, waiting for a ship. At last the troops were ready to embark for Cuba. Kit saw the newspaper men depart, and realized that she was being left behind purposely. Finally, however, she was able to get passage on a Red Cross ship under the protection of Clara Barton, founder of the American Red Cross.

Despite the aggravating delays and obvious snubs, Kit persevered and eventually her determination won her universal admiration. The *Daily Mail* in London, England, wrote her up as a heroine in an article "The Lady War Correspondent" and described her as "a tall, healthy, youngish lady, with a quiet self-reliant manner, an alert, intelligent, enterprising look and the prettiest touch of the Irish brogue." In the United States, she was hailed as a hero and was invited to lecture on the war, which she declined to do because she viewed the war as a case of total mismanagement.

Her colleagues were impressed also by her abilities as a journalist. As one wrote, "There is no question that her department was the most distinctive on the paper, perhaps the most widely read in Canadian journalism. She had humour mixed with tenderness and a very sharp wit." Praise such as this did much to help open the doors of journalism to other women by reducing the prejudice among men and by inspiring other women to follow her example. On a more personal level, however, it provided Kit with a sense of fulfilment born of achievement.

The same combination of need and determination motivated another well-known woman journalist. "Ma" Murray, born into a working-class family, went to work early and continued through the years until she, too, made a mark for herself in the rough, male-dominated world of newspapers.

Margaret Murray

Soon after Margaret Murray, or "Ma" as she later became known, started work for the Shipley Saddlery Company in Kansas City, she began tucking notes in with the invoices for saddles shipped off to cowboys in Alberta. Her idea resulted in a large correspondence between the "Shipley girls" and the company's northern customers. It was not long before the six girls had collected everything from pictures, walrus mustaches, stetsons, and buffalo coats, to invitations to come out and visit, not to mention several marriage proposals. To someone with Margaret's curiosity and spunk, it was too good an opportunity to pass up. In 1912, she set out for Canada to look over the prospects, quite convinced that one at least would "pan out."

En route, she ran out of money and had to take a series of jobs in Vancouver. She did everything from making beds in a hotel in exchange for her accommodation, to selling subscriptions to the province's first labour newspaper, the *B.C. Federation* – a job for which she soon revealed she had a considerable talent. When a doctor demanded to know just why he should invest in a labour paper, she rallied unabashedly: "Doctor, you look like a man of great understanding and I'm sure among your patients will be many who are very interested in the labour movement right now, and they would be bound to appreciate..." Soon afterwards, Margaret was offered a permanent job as bookkeeper for the *Chinook*, a small weekly newspaper in South Vancouver. She accepted, but not before talking the boss into giving her $15 a week instead of his original offer of $12. As the seventh of nine children born to poor Irish immigrant farmers, Margaret had learned early to look out for herself.

Margaret found working for the *Chinook* exciting. Although she admittedly knew nothing about it, she had a natural ability for newspaper work. In the years since she had applied for her first job as a housemaid at only fourteen, she had developed from what she later described as an "awkward lump" to a lively, fun-loving, attractive young woman. Not only did people want to meet and talk to her, but she genuinely liked people. Moreover, she had an avid curiosity about everything, an attribute for which she thanked her public school teacher back in Kansas. "She gave me a book in 1901 and told me to learn it all by heart even if it was only the Almanac...I inherited my curiosity from that."

Margaret threw herself into newspaper work with the same enthusiasm and initiative that her prompted her to enroll in a cram secretarial course in Freemont, Nebraska, where she arranged to pay her tuition by washing dishes. A year later she graduated with top grades and had no trouble getting the position at the Shipley Saddlery Company in Kansas City.

Although she was officially hired as a bookkeeper, Margaret's outgoing, friendly personality made it only a matter of time before she was eagerly taking on all sorts of extra jobs. She collected accounts and managed to keep customers happy; she read proofs and she began to do a little reporting. While out collecting accounts Margaret had made friends with people such as the clergymen and their wives and the purchasing agents, all of whom gave her local news and community announcements which she wrote up for the *Chinook*. Fellow employees at the *Chinook* were quick to recognize Margaret's dedication to her job. "If picking up the district news meant sitting down under the correspondent's holly tree and sipping raspberry cider, then cider was Margaret's drink," one of them remembered. Another recalled that after her boss recommended that Margaret use the public library for background material on people she was interviewing, Margaret put in many nights there acquiring some of the education she had missed by leaving school at fourteen.

Once she began reporting, one thing led to another, for she had hardly sorted out the political parties in Canada than she was out covering local political meetings. It was her write-up of one such affair which introduced Margaret to libel problems. After a particularly heated ratepayers' meeting, she captured the emotion of the night if not the facts and wrote that they threw the Reeve out the window.

The *Chinook* editor, as many editors would be forced to do in the future, sent her to argue her own case with the publisher, George Murray. "Boy, these Canadians sure take themselves serious," she wrote home to Kansas that week. "But anyway I like my job. My boss is a nice young man, a little vague and annoying but real handsome." While Margaret admitted her boss was "real handsome" and that his loyalty to friends took her breath away, she added "he is too wrapped up in his work to notice me."

It was not until after Margaret gave up her job and went to Calgary to check on "her cowboys" that George Murray realized how indispensable she was not only to the paper but to him as well. When she returned to Vancouver suddenly to do some business for a friend, George met her at the station proclaiming loudly that the *Chinook* was a morgue without her. That night he took her to dinner and proposed. Margaret was overwhelmed.

> Marry you? Me?...Me a clerk and you a publisher. I only went to grade four...you've got nice manners and good taste – you want to be a senator for goodness sakes! Your folks are well off. Look at me. Me a Catholic and you – Glory be to God! I couldn't be anything else but what I am. I couldn't be a Presbyterian. It would be like cutting off my hands ...What would my mother say? And what would your aunts say?

"Well your mother isn't marrying me and you're not marrying my aunts, so why bring it up?" George pointed out. His persistent arguments persuaded her to overlook their differences in background, and they were married in February 1913, less than a year after she had arrived in Vancouver.

At first, George's two maiden aunts disapproved of their nephew's "Kansas farm girl" and made little effort to disguise it. Prim and proper, they had both trained as nurses and persisted in referring to all non-nurses as "the laity," and in dropping in for weekly sanitary inspection tours of the young couple's flat. Uncharacteristically subdued by this formidable pair, Margaret was still too intimidated and impressed with George's family to object and endured their interference, even allowing them to select a nurse and doctor for the delivery of her first child, Georgina, in 1914.

From the beginning, the young Murrays faced financial problems. Money was scarce and the advertising in the *Chinook* dropped to a mere trickle as the building boom in Vancouver ended. The outbreak of war in 1914 aggravated the problem. George cut back on his staff and freelanced to support his new family. Margaret helped with accounts after their second child, Dan, was born in 1916, but even her careful bookkeeping could not stave off poverty. Accustomed to hard times, Margaret tried to make the best of it. "George, supper is on the table," she used to say. "You've got the imagination in the family, so you can pretend this rice is pheasant under glass. Actually, it's better for you." In those years the menu varied little – boiled rice and raisins with brown sugar and milk, brown homemade bread and blackberry jam, no butter, and tea.

As their finances did not improve, the Murrays decided that the best thing to do was to take up homesteading on the shores of Burrard Inlet which, at that time, was still not connected to Vancouver by road or bridge. In 1916 they built a tarpaper frame cottage, cleared an acre or so of land, and managed to grow enough in the scrubby soil to survive while they waited for better times. But things did not improve, and George was finally forced to sell the *Chinook* and go to work fulltime on the *Province*, leaving Margaret and the children all week at the homestead while he stayed with his aunts. Margaret coped cheerfully with her isolated and primitive surroundings, clearing land, splitting shakes, picking berries, and, later, building their house. Only when George finally became managing editor of the Vancouver *Morning Sun* could he afford to move his family back to the city.

When the Murrays returned to Vancouver, Margaret returned to work. She started *Country Life in B.C.*, a magazine that tried to provide British Columbia with some insight into what went on beyond the Vancouver city limits, a part of the land that was becoming her passion. All went well for eight years until *Country Life in B.C.* had to close because of the Depression. At the same time, George's salary was cut by half and once again the Murrays returned to their homestead. As Margaret said later,

> What else could we do? There we were in Vancouver without any money, with a lot of big ideas and a lot of big debts to go with them. I was...trying to collect old accounts I knew we'd never get, and thinking about how we were going to educate our two youngsters and just eat.

The years passed but the effects of the Depression persisted. George and Margaret made plans to start a paper in which they could express their own political views without interference from editors, and George wanted to enter politics himself. In the 1933 provincial election he was nominated as the Liberal candidate for Lillooet and, after three months of hard campaigning, was elected. In those three months Margaret handed out 3,000 blotters, walked and rode the Pacific Great Eastern railway track from Squamish to Shalalth, met everyone, and forever after remembered who had rust in the wheat, erysipelas in the hogs, or milk-leg after the last baby. Her personality made her a great asset during her husband's campaigns among the down-to-earth, practical, and unsophisticated northerners.

After the election, Margaret changed from campaigner to newspaper woman, pouring her energy into helping start the paper she and George had dreamed of ever since the sale of the *Chinook*. Throughout George's campaign, both of them had learned what they could about the district and had collected enough information and local colour to start a weekly paper in Lillooet, British Columbia, fill it with some of the most colourful journalism in the West, and make it pay. It was no easy task, for in 1934 Lillooet presented problems to anyone with no cash who tried to start any business, let alone a paper. The small frontier town, some two hundred miles north of Vancouver, had an uncertain mail service, bad transportation facilities, and a meagre population. The Murrays were well aware of these risks after their travels in the district but, as Margaret put it: "We cared about its future and its potential and placed the present difficulties second." Recognizing the importance of advertising to get the paper launched, Margaret went from door to door in Lillooet selling all the advertising space she could, then went to Vancouver to persuade wholesalers, mining people, and other suppliers of goods and services to Lillooet to advertise in the paper. Not until her orders were filled did she hurry back to Lillooet where, in March 1934, the *Bridge River-Lillooet News* began with Margaret virtually in charge.

With George away most of the time in the British Columbia Legislature, Margaret often had to be publisher, editor, and business manager, and for the first time in her life her free, lurid prose appeared unedited by her more articulate and cautious husband. "I had a chance to come into my own," she explained recently. The fact is she had little choice. Someone had to support the family as George's salary as an M.P.L. was only $1,200 a year. It wasn't long before Margaret Murray had made a mark on the community, delighting, amusing, and infuriating the paper's increasing readership. Many became devotees of the lively paper mainly because of the editor's irreverent tone, libellous comments, blunt statements, and shocking subject matter – all delivered in a never-ending stream of atrocious grammar and spelling. Words like "damshur," "craporini," and "snaffoo" peppered her writing and endeared her to hundreds. To many, her prose captured the individualism of the frontier with its defiance of convention and laws, its tough, raw atmosphere, and its practical, ambitious approach to life.

Margaret seemed compelled to stir up trouble or, as she put it, "to examine everything and tell things as they were." But without the editing of her husband, the free expression of her opinions soon left a trail of complaints and legal battles in their wake. "My client," Angelo Branca, a struggling young Vancouver criminal lawyer wrote to the *News* in 1936, "is not a crooked horse-trader and he is not a gypsy. He therefore demands a full retraction for your statement regarding him in the last issue." When the retraction was not made, the paper was forced to pay costs. Another time Margaret ran into trouble when she started publishing the guest registry at the Mines Hotel in Lillooet. "It seemed like a good idea," she said, until she found herself sending copies of the paper off to divorce lawyers and receiving requests like the following: "Please send us the April 15 issue of the *News*. We are interested in the guest registry at the Mines Hotel. Our client is anxious to secure the report that her husband registered himself and wife at the Mines Hotel that week. Having just returned from six months in the East, she is, as you will understand, puzzled." Margaret agreed to hold back on that part of her social column but she found it harder to keep from making libellous comments.

Reporting the acquittal of a man charged with murder, she ran the headline, ANOTHER MURDERER GOES FREE, and when writing up a violent death, she wrote the accused "came running up the hill to the police with the news that his wife was lying there with her head chopped off." Margaret concluded that the husband would probably be sent to a mental hospital. Nothing was sacred to Margaret's pen; she could always smell a good story. Once, for instance, she happened upon the public health officer making his first trip down the valley.

"Pull up a minute, Curly, let's see what's going on," she said, hopping out in time to catch a fight between two women. "Believe me, Mrs. Skillicorn, your privy ain't no honey pot either," the wife of the hotel proprietor was saying. "It may not be a honey pot, Mrs. Mac," replied Thyra Skillicorn, a former nurse, "but if you put lime in yours..."

"Ladies, ladies," pleaded the Sanitary Inspector. Right there, Margaret had the beginning of a good earthy report on the sanitation situation in the valley.

With copy such as this, Margaret's sales soared. Most readers got the "chuckle every week and a belly laugh (or ache) once a month" promised on the paper's masthead on a money-back guarantee. But since Margaret got many of these chuckles at the expense of other people, she amassed an impressive array of enemies over the years, including victims who resorted to various and sometimes colourful means in their attempts to stem the never-ending flow. One woman threatened Margaret with a horse whip; others broke into her office to destroy editorials before they went to print; many insulted and shunned her. All, of course, to no avail. The benign-looking, greying, bespectacled editor merely regarded criticism, threats, and unpopularity as occupational hazards, and more often than not got good mileage out of such incidents in one of her later columns. "I don't mind," she claimed, "after all it's a poor turkey that can't pack a few lice." Her opponents at last realized that their anger would not stop the torrent of words that continued to flow from Margaret's pen without heed to punctuation, grammar, spelling, or libel laws.

As long as Margaret was running the paper there was always some problem. In the early days the paper had to be published in Vancouver, which meant mailing the copy in time for publication every Wednesday (late news could be wired the day before) and then arranging for the bundles of papers to be loaded onto a train-boat to Squamish from where they went by rail to Lillooet. This arrangement lasted for two years until the Murrays converted an abandoned building on the main street in Lillooet into offices and a shop, installed their own printing press, and made the upstairs their living quarters. Since by that time, both Murray children were working on the paper, the arrangement proved economical as well as convenient.

Living so close to the business was almost a necessity for Margaret Murray, for whatever happened she always turned it into news. Even when a neighbour's eight-year-old boy had his skull punctured in a sleighing accident, Margaret stopped only to gather up a feather tick off her own bed to make him comfortable in the car before she hurried to her typewriter to get the story: "Last night in Egan's Alley, tragedy raced and overtook an eight-year-old sleighrider..."

About this time a Toronto writer, Earl Beattie, dubbed the infamous and, by now, middle-aged editor "Ma" Murray and the name stuck. Even Margaret, who loathed the name at first, in time took to signing her column "Ma Murray."

When, in 1942, Lillooet became a centre for 3,800 interned Japanese Canadians, things got "too crowded" for Margaret. "It's pure blankety-blank that I left because I didn't like the Japanese," she says now, with her usual eloquence. At the time, though, she was upset and, as usual, did not hide her feelings. "We had never minced words concerning our fear of the Japanese Empire or their people in Vancouver. People soon forget, but we were not alone in this fear."

In Lillooet, where businesses suffering from the effects of the war were only too happy to accept the unexpected trade from the Japanese, Margaret's views were not appreciated. "You better look out, Margaret Murray," one man warned her, "or the people around here will tar and feather you...Shut your mouth down there at the paper or leave town." And she did.

As their new home, the Murrays chose Fort St. John, some 450 miles south of Whitehorse, in the lush agricultural lands of the Peace River Valley. In 1942 the town was at the height of a short-lived period of prosperity brought about by the arrival of some 10,000 American troops, who had been sent to cut the trail through the bush from Fort St. John to Whitehorse, to provide a route "over the top of the world" for American supplies to Russia.

Margaret had discovered the town by accident. She had managed to get a pass from the Northern Alberta Railways to Dawson Creek, an area she had always wanted to see, and en route she happened to stop off at Fort St. John. She immediately noticed the impact the sudden boom had made on the quiet little town and its citizens. There was an instant market for everything – including a newspaper. The excitement in Fort St. John was contagious and infected Margaret who arrived home overflowing with plans to start a paper there. George Murray, who knew the place too, was just as enthusiastic. The fact that Margaret was fifty-five and he was fifty-six, seemed irrelevant. They both recognized that Fort St. John was now the frontier and that was where they had to be. Long before he had moved to Lillooet, George had dreamed of opening up Canada's northlands. "Put relief dollars to work extending the railway," he used to urge the Legislature at Victoria, pleading that "riches beyond the dreams of Midas lie at our backdoor." No one but his wife had listened then, and, as Georgina pointed out somewhat bitterly, it was American money and initiative that opened up the North.

It took 135 million American dollars to provide a defence road to Alaska, and waken Canada's Pacific province to its own wealth. It took war correspondents and magazine writers from the United States to convince British Columbians that here indeed was a magnificent country, and it was theirs.

Preparations for the move took more than a year, a year spent bringing out a meagre paper at Lillooet, living for news from their children who were both overseas, and making plans.

The Alaska Highway News finally appeared in 1944. This time Margaret was helped by her husband, temporarily at least, as he had been defeated after eight years in the British Columbia Legislature. Margaret had not helped his position in the party or his campaign since she refused adamantly to make her editorial policy toe the party line. Even during the campaign, she often wrote vitriolic editorials against the Liberals. "What are we coming to?" she wrote after the Liberal premier had sympathized with soldiers stationed in Nanaimo, who had complained of getting tired of apples. "It smacks of senile decay on the part of the Premier, panty-waist fortitude on the part of the soldiers..."

"In the name of reason what are you trying to do to me?" George Murray wrote angrily from Victoria. But his pleas were to no avail, for in the next week's issue Margaret decried the money the provincial government had spent on education during the late thirties and pointed out that in spite of it all "little

Johnny [still] couldn't read in 1940." Like so many other victims of her attacks, George, too, gave up trying to dictate editorial policy to his wife. "Why shouldn't I have spoken out," she asked her critics. "My husband was always Liberal but I have an open mind."

Neither of the Murrays had time to regret George's defeat. They had no sooner got the paper going in 1944 than the U.S. troops stationed along the Alaska Highway pulled out, leaving the town to pick itself up after its short-lived prosperity. Business fell off at the dance halls, pubs, movies, and drug stores, cutting advertising and leaving little news to write about for the few people left to read the fledgling paper. Ironically, it was this crisis that made Ma Murray famous across the country. In a desperate effort to fill her paper, she poured much of herself into it, confessing only later that "there was so little news that I had to make it myself – and that's how I've got my reputation." As in Lillooet, half the town of Fort St. John loved her and half hated her, but she still made them laugh. Early in 1958, for instance, there was an acute water shortage in town and, in the lead editorial, she told people to "only flush for No. 2, curtail bathing to the Saturday night tub, and go back to the old washrag, which could always move a lot of B.O. if applied often enough." Some people were shocked, others laughed, but all conserved water, reducing the drain on the local reservoir by one hundred gallons in a single night.

Again, the Murrays faced innumerable problems in the early years of the *News*. The heavy presses could not be transported over the rough, uncompleted road, and so once again they had to put up with the inconvenience of publishing their paper in Vancouver. This time they had to fly their copy to Vancouver, then ship back the bundles of newspapers midweek in time for Thursday distribution. The arrangement worked most weeks, but on occasion the entire edition would end up in St. John's, Newfoundland, or St. John, New Brunswick, and at times would disappear altogether.

Of all the political in-fighting Margaret did in her columns and editorials, over the years Premier W.A.C. Bennett and his government emerged as her biggest target. Except for her one short flirtation with the Social Credit Party, Ma was always a staunch Liberal and, as such, decried the long rule of former Premier Bennett, whom she detested. On one occasion Premier Bennett himself tried to win her over with sweetness and greeted her with a kiss, somewhat to the astonishment of reporters. When asked later on television if she had kissed the Premier, she replied, "He may have kissed me but I didn't kiss the old blankety-blank back." Later, in 1966, the Premier tried again to win her over. This time, acting on rumours that Mrs. Murray was going soft, he stopped off at her office in Lillooet during an election campaign. Margaret, then seventy-nine, wasn't there, but when she heard of his visit she declared to all who would listen that he could go "right to hell."

Ma Murray's feelings were as strong as her language when it came to politics. She became so irate when the Liberals and Conservatives formed the Coalition Party in 1945 that she ran as the Social Credit candidate in the Peace River riding, shocking and irritating her Liberal family and friends. Her daughter Georgina heard about it during a stopover in Toronto on her way home from the war and thought her mother had "lost her wits," probably because she had been working on the newspaper too long without help. Her son, who fought with his mother at the best of times, was then acting as the temporary editor of the *Bridge River-Lillooet News.* He announced angrily on the front page that "Mrs. Margaret Murray has nothing to do with the editing of this paper" and denounced her copy as "gunk, needing hours of editing before it could be published." George Murray, long resigned to his wife's blatant disregard for what other people thought or felt about her, blamed her latest blow to his career on "modern woman."

Margaret, overlooking the scandal she had created, went about her riding holding forth at dozens of farm gatherings. Knowing little about her new party's policies, she shrugged off difficult questions saying she "hadn't had time to go into it" but she was sure "it was good for Alberta." In this manner she sailed through twenty-nine meetings in twenty days, dared her opponents to meet her in open debate, and turned out a steady stream of blistering editorials. People lined up outside the Carlsonia Theatre in Fort St. John just to hear her, but the few votes she won revealed that, apart from the residents of her hometown, no one took her seriously.

Her temporary fling with the Social Credit Party did not go unnoticed at Liberal headquarters in Ottawa. When her husband sought the Liberal nomination for the Cariboo riding in the election of 1949, Ottawa bluntly informed him in a telegram that "he would never make it." Ma, who had signed for and opened the telegram, went on to read their explanation with increasing anger: "We learn your wife was a Social Credit nominee in 1945. She's fouled up your chances, so no dice on expenses!" Before her husband came home, Ma had wired back: "Hustle the contribution. The campaign is on as I'm going to win this seat and I'll have 1,600 of a majority." She signed George's name, sent it back to headquarters in Ottawa, and only told George weeks later when they could see victory in the offing.

After George won, the couple headed for Ottawa leaving their son, Dan, to run the paper. At least that is what he thought he had returned from California to do, but Margaret never gave him a moment's peace: "Daniel Murray, don't you leave out one single line of this... Dan, don't change one word..." "The paper was my heritage only if I conformed to her iron will. And I couldn't do this," Dan said later. Georgina recalls that her mother started giving him her orders the Sunday before she left and Dan decided to go over the subscription list. "Hundreds of people had not paid. He was knocking them off right and left...Mother was weeping tears. This one had milk-leg after the last baby. That fellow had erysipelas in the hogs...Dan had no charity, no heart." By the time they came home for their first visit, Dan had packed up and gone, leaving Ma no choice but to stay in Fort St. John when her husband returned to Ottawa. Her decision met with no opposition, as

George Murray realized it would be useless to bring in an outsider to run the paper. Although not her son's idea of a businesswoman, Ma Murray's reputation and success as a controversial editor made it almost imperative that she stay on the job. Besides, she thought Ottawa conversation "too damned dull."

In 1958, the Murrays sold the *Alaska Highway News* to Georgina and Dan, who was persuaded to come back as part owner. They asked only ten cents on the dollar, turning down an offer of $50,000 just "to keep the paper in the family." That, at least, is Margaret's version of the story. According to Georgina, the relationships among the four Murrays were often tense and turbulent, mainly because Ma and Dan fought constantly. "The price we paid for the paper was fair but not a giveaway as she let others think," Dan said when he finally bought control of the paper. Dan had little time for his mother's disregard for the financial side of the business, while she was equally critical of his tactics: "He is the natural sequence to the union of two people who did not really think that money was important. The swing of the pendulum. Cut off my hands at the wrists if I know who in the world he takes after."

After Dan took over running the paper at Fort St. John, Margaret and George returned to Lillooet where they were able to buy back the little paper they had started there. The old shop was closed, and the machines were covered with dirt and rust, so the paper had to be printed in Vancouver as it had been years before. Nonetheless, the Murrays were content to be back in business in Lillooet. George, however, died in August 1961, and once again Margaret had to carry on alone. She surprised and touched her readers by writing her husband's obituary herself, although she had to have them hold the paper a day so she could muster the strength to do it. "He was our life, our light and our inspiration...and our flapdoodle vernacular or daring courage only came from the inward security he gave us."

Ma Murray went on alone to shock, delight, and infuriate her readers. At eighty years of age, she showed the same sense for news as she always had. When she received a phone call from Simma Holt requesting her to write her own obituary for *The Sun*, she quickly grasped the potential for a story in the macabre request and asked for it in writing. She published it the day after she received it and then turned the incident into one of the most amusing columns of her weekly "Chat Out of the Old Bag":

> And what do we do when a distinguished dame like Simma Holt calls us from *The Sun* and asks us in all sobriety if we will write our own obituary and have it ready for them, and now is that a hint that this old gal can now go out and get herself run over by some truck driver when we feel already like we are flattened lower than a snake's belly by the people who keep our life one jump ahead of the sheriff, getting the mazuma to keep this rag a-going and filling it with the same corny stuff that Simma thinks ought to be preserved in *The Sun* for posterity in a self-written obituary.

As she had predicted, columnists picked up the subject of her self-written obituary and once again Ma's latest venture was dinner-table conversation across Canada.

Even though she has written her own obituary and could die with the assurance that Canadians would be duly informed of the role she has played in the newspaper world and in the development of the British Columbia hinterland, Margaret Murray continues to make news one way or another. She has appeared on several television shows as one of the vanishing breed of colourful personalities in the newspaper business and as a spokesman for the hurly-burly rough days of the North. Since selling the *Bridge River-Lillooet News* in 1973, she has been working on a book on sex, which will no doubt vindicate her claim that "there could be a little good still left in the old mare."

Helen MacGill at her graduation from Trinity College.

CHAPTER FIVE

The Doors of Academe

Towards the end of the nineteenth century, some women tried to go beyond teaching and missionary work and break into the world of higher education, only to discover that the doors of Canadian universities were closed to them. In 1882, Mount Allison University in New Brunswick set a precedent by permitting women to enroll in Arts, and by the end of the decade the majority of Canadian universities had opened their doors to women, although not without considerable resistance. Writing of the university climate she faced at the time she herself had struggled to be admitted, Judge Helen MacGill observed, "The university classroom – a seat for the development of the mind – was a milieu in which women...seemed startlingly out of place. [To most Victorians, the] development of a girl's mind was superfluous; motherhood was considered her only important function, and family life her only satisfactory destiny. To send her to college would make her unfit for a passive role as wife and mother, and develop in her an objectivity which, though thought admirable in a man, was then considered awkward, unpleasant, and masculine in a woman."

Nowhere was this conservatism more apparent than among

the staid maiden teachers in ladies' academies who carefully preserved traditional attitudes towards the role of women. Elizabeth Veals was typical of this sort of woman teacher whose Victorian views on education perpetuated female dependence. Miss Veals' ability to attract pupils to her school on the promise of nothing more than a chance to dabble in a few "cultural pursuits" is an indication of the strong hold that the Victorian ideal of the model young lady still had on society before the turn of the century.

Miss Veals was born in Canada during the nineteenth century (in keeping with Victorian propriety no record remains of her date of birth). She began her career in education as a governess and later founded Glen Mawr School for Girls in Toronto. The school's curriculum, which reflected the views of its principal, was designed to "give all Canadian girls...the poise of English gentlewomen." Miss Veals taught her girls various drawing-room accomplishments, including deportment, etiquette, and music, which more than satisfied her pupils' parents, many of whom came from the growing commercial class and still harboured memories of their own harsh working-class past and they had no desire to train their daughters to work. Moreover, to be able to afford to send one's daughter to a ladies' academy was a symbol of social prestige and wealth. For Anglo-Saxon parents, many of these schools had the added appeal of being patterned on schools in the "Mother country."

The parents' insistence on a Victorian education for their daughters left the teachers of these establishments little choice but to abide by the traditional curriculum if they wished to keep their jobs which, as was usually the case, were their only means of support. Even such an intelligent woman as Mary Ellen Knox, the principal of Havergal College in Toronto, who had obtained her own education after a struggle against traditional views on education for women, did little to encourage her students to persevere with academic studies that would prepare them for a career outside the home or provide them with the prerequisites for university entrance.

Mary Ellen Knox was born in England in 1859, the daughter of a vicar. Her father had little money to bequeath to his daughter and decided to provide her with some form of practical training. He tutored her first for the certificates required for an elementary school teacher and later for her examinations at Oxford, despite the fact that at that time the admission of women to all universities was still a matter of considerable controversy and regulations at Oxford limited enrollment to men only. The Knoxes remained resolute and eventually Oxford compromised by admitting women not to the public examinations but to equivalent examinations conducted by the university. Ellen's excellent results disproved the contention that women could not bear the strain of examinations, but after her academic success she seemed content to slip back into the conventional role of the spinster daughter of a vicar. She became a teacher at the Cheltenham School for Girls and, in 1894, accepted the position of first principal of Havergal Hall (now College) in Toronto. By choosing a career in the conservative world of schools for genteel young ladies, Miss Knox cut herself off from any opportunity to further the cause of women's education, as any radical move in this controversial area would probably have cost her her job.

The weight of Miss Knox's academic qualifications added a certain prestige to her position but, in practice, she brought little, if any, change to the conventional curriculum for young ladies at that time. It was basically designed to equip young girls for the role of the virtuous, charming, middle-class wife and mother who knows how to converse superficially on a wide range of topics but who knows too little to do anything else, and so has to remain dependent on her husband.

Despite this limited education and the attitudes that perpetuated it, a few graduates of such institutions – women such as Helen MacGill – grew up to challenge the status quo, only to discover that their poor academic qualifications severely handicapped their quest for a higher education.

Helen MacGill

Born in Hamilton in 1864, Helen Gregory had received a "genteel education" at the hands of a Miss Frick whom she described as a "decayed gentlewoman...whose knowledge and range of school subjects was sadly limited." But, as Helen explained later, since weakness in academic subjects was considered pardonable and even engaging in women, her parents were not concerned. What did matter was that she should attend a private school. Despite the excellent public schools established by Ryerson by mid-century, her father, Silas Gregory, insisted that a gentleman's daughter should not be educated at the public expense nor in the company of children from the industrial classes. At sixteen, Helen "came out," wearing a full dress with bustle and train and eighteen-button gloves, and was given the privilege of receiving "cards" in her own name for the round of local balls and "at homes" that comprised much of upper-class life in Hamilton in those days.

Coming from this background, Helen's decision to pursue a career would have been strange indeed had it not been for her extraordinarily modern-minded mother who openly championed liberal ideas, especially on the status of women. Emma Gregory firmly believed that women should have a voice in public matters, should vote in elections and hold public office – all ideas which were considered extremely radical in Canada in the 1870's. It was not surprising then, that Helen rejected the blueprint for a traditional future in order to pursue a career as a concert pianist. Her rigidly conformist father and grandparents were scandalized, fearing that such a lowerclass and unconventional move would jeopardize Helen's chances of making a good marriage. But Helen solicited her mother's support, and together they persuaded the apprehensive family that the study of music would not ruin her marriage prospects. "An artist," her mother pointed out in her defence, "does not forfeit gentility." Eventually, her doting father was persuaded to take her to play for Arthur Fisher, a well-known Toronto teacher, who immediately entered her in his classes which prepared candidates for the Music Baccalaureate examinations.

After studying and practising for eight hours a day Helen had surprised and delighted her parents by topping her class in her first-year examinations only to learn that her fellow male candidates would be eligible for a degree at the end of the three-year course whereas she, who had so clearly demonstrated a superior talent, would have to make do with a certificate. She had never thought seriously about women's rights until that time, but there was no way that she would accept and be content with the certificate granted women for successfully completing the same exams for which men were granted a degree. As a result, she resolved to petition the university administrators to consider the question of granting women degrees in music. She soon realized, however, that this body of men were not going to give way easily, if at all.

Rather than give up her fight, Helen enlisted the support of her influential grandfather, Miles O'Reilly, Q.C., Judge of the District of Gore, and, partly as a result of the pressure he exerted, Trinity finally capitulated in December 1885 with a declaration that it would grant women degrees in all faculties on equal terms with men. The declaration, however, was not without a catch: women were to be admitted to the university *only* if they had passed their matriculation exam. This new regulation seemed clearly calculated to keep women from invading the male precincts of Trinity, for the acadamies for young ladies where middle- and upper-class girls were educated gave scant attention to the subjects that were needed to pass a matriculation exam.

Helen, who was already preparing for her final examinations in music, was appalled at first by this unexpected obstacle. At Miss Frick's she had studied no Latin, no Greek, no mathematics, no science, and had touched on geography and history only superficially – all subjects required for matriculation. Furthermore, she had been out of school for eight years and had never really been studious. Nonetheless, as an eager, ambitious twenty-one-year old, Helen saw it as a challenge. She decided she would write and pass her music examinations first and, with that behind her, would then apply herself to cramming for the matriculation exams. Her single-mindedness worked, for she passed both sets of exams even though she had spent only one summer studying for her matriculation. In the fall of 1886, Helen and another woman in her class became the first women to be awarded Bachelor of Music degrees in Canada.

Helen had little time to rest on her laurels. She had already applied to the Faculty of Arts at Trinity only to find yet another obstacle confronting her. Although Trinity had changed its regulations to admit women, its *Calendar* of 1885 stated that for women "attendance at lectures will not be required." In other words, women students were expected to do all their preparation as best they could outside the college. Helen's application to Trinity was refused and once again her grandfather was called on to rally support from his influential friends and acquaintances. As a result of the pressure they exerted, Helen's application was finally accepted.

Even after she had been admitted, Helen's problems were far from over. As she was the only woman student, her arrival caused quite a sensation at the sedate Toronto college. Reactions to the slight, oval-faced, pretty intruder were mixed. Her admirers dubbed her a "pocket Venus" and allowed that she could be "frightfully clever," but others felt threatened by her presence. The situation placed her under tremendous pressure, particularly as her admission to Trinity had attracted considerable public attention and had aroused the wrath of those who viewed the education of women with alarm.

These views were shared by some Trinity academics; one professor resigned, but finding that his resignation was accepted, swallowed his pride and returned. When he discovered that Helen was one of his students, he informed the class that while he could not refuse her admission to his lectures, "he deplored her presence and considered himself in no sense responsible for her progress in Deductive and Inductive Logic, Metaphysics and Ethics." Then he placed a chair apart from the group, and invited her to occupy it for that and all subsequent lectures. Aside from blushing, Helen refrained from showing any reaction at the time; at the end of the year, however, she gave the professor an eloquent rebuke by taking first class honours in his course. Later, she won the respect of the entire faculty and student body by graduating *cum laude.*

At convocation in June 1889, Helen Gregory became Trinity's first woman graduate in Arts. When she stepped on the dais to receive her degree, the whole gallery broke into "The Merriest Girl That's Out." Despite many predictions to the contrary, study had not made Helen "dull, docile or literal-minded." After three years at college, Helen was as lively and quick-witted as ever.

Helen's struggle to break into the world of higher learning and her ensuing academic success had made her believe more strongly than ever in equality for the sexes. "A woman should be an equally active and responsible sharer in the equal partnership of marriage and should be given complete freedom in applying her talents." After her graduation, she was not content to abandon her intellectual pursuits. For the first time in years she was free of exams and practising schedules and had the time to travel. While visiting Montreal where her mother was attending a meeting, Helen joined the Quebec Press Association as one of its first women members. A little later, on a trip to Washington, D.C. to stay with relatives, she met John Brisban Walker, the editor of *The Cosmopolitan,* a magazine then covering the political field. Noticing the young lady's intellect, Walker invited her to send in articles – an offer that was to launch Helen on a life-long career as a part-time journalist.

By the spring of 1890, she had so impressed Walker with the searching quality of her mind and her clear literary style that he decided that the opening of the Diet (parliament) in Japan in December 1890 was "just the thing for the lively, observant Miss Gregory" to cover. To the horror of her relatives who thought it "a preposterous proposal for a young unmarried girl," Helen accepted the assignment. Not only her family, but the public and even the reputedly open-minded press looked askance at the assignment for, in 1890, the Orient was still very much a place of dark mysteries and the idea of a young girl travelling there alone savoured of impropriety as well as flamboyant recklessness. Even the editors of the Toronto *Globe* reflected this conventional attitude for, when Helen tried to convince them to buy some stories she planned to write on the development of the Canadian west after the completion of the C.P.R., they thought the project "too arduous and mature especially [for] an elegant young thing with big blue eyes and small face."

Helen had originally got the idea of writing on the West from an old family friend, Sir John A. Macdonald. He had suggested to her that if she would visit and write about some of the outlying settlements on her journey across the Canadian West, he would arrange railway passes and all official aid. However, even the Prime Minister's confidence in this young woman's abilities did not impress the skeptical editors at the *Globe*. Only when they learned that two well-known American magazines had already hired her as correspondent to cover the opening of the first Japanese Diet, did they agree to buy some of her proposed stories.

Skeptical as her parents were about their daughter's latest venture, they could do little to stop her. Helen simply refused to be dissuaded, arguing that despite her intellectual freedom, she had led a sheltered life and now longed for adventure. She spoke so passionately against "sitting on the sidelines while life passed her by" that once again she succeeded in winning her family's approval – a decision they were soon to regret bitterly.

On her assignment in the West, Helen paid as little heed to convention as she had in considering the trip in the first place. She stopped in Winnipeg and filed a story, then continued on to Deloraine to stay with her brother and his wife, from whose home she intended to make day trips to nearby immigrant settlements. Since there were no roads across the Prairie, Helen's brother quite innocently arranged for a friend to accompany his sister and act as a guide. Helen was delighted with the arrangement, especially since her guide turned out to be a tall, good-looking westerner of twenty-three. Lee Flesher rode like an Indian, was a crack shot with a revolver, and had tremendous vitality, strength, and high spirits. To Helen, he seemed the very personification of the West – of its free, wide-open spaces, and the energy, confidence, and enthusiasm it inspired. Indeed, Lee and the West seemed to promise the adventure she had been seeking.

Just one week after first setting eyes on him, Trinity College's first woman B.A. and the daughter of one of Hamilton's leading families married her rancher-guide in a secret ceremony which she described as "an ecstasy important to themselves alone to be announced joyously later." The secret was not kept for long. A few weeks later the local doctor innocently mentioned he had had a visit from "the young Flesher couple who are expecting a baby." Helen, suddenly realizing her thoughtlessness, was forced to confront her shocked and bitter relatives. Helen's brother felt his friend Lee had betrayed his trust, Helen's new in-laws were offended at having been left out, and as might be expected, Helen's own parents in Hamilton were appalled at the nature and the extraordinary circumstances of her marriage, which of course gave rise to all sorts of embarrassing rumours.

But Helen had little time to brood over the feelings she had hurt. She had been steadily writing stories that captured the feeling of excitement in the developing West where hundreds of settlers of different races, backgrounds, and creeds struggled to adjust to life in a new and foreign land. Helen never considered changing her plans: she had an assignment to do and, pregnant or not, she would complete it. And so, in the late summer of 1890, Helen left her husband of five weeks and set off for Japan.

In Tokyo, Helen's letters of introduction brought her invitations to a seemingly endless round of balls and dinners.

People were eager to have their customs interpreted sympathetically and went to endless trouble to explain things to the visiting journalist. The articles Helen wrote on the opening of the Japanese Diet and those on the Japanese people established her reputation as a journalist of note. Editors praised her "fluent and prolific" style, incisiveness and vivid imagery. Her stories were marked by a refreshing lack of Victorian sentimentality and ponderousness, a characteristic that placed them in sharp contrast to other 1890 bylines and won her a large following of readers as well as the admiration of many editors across the country.

On her return in January 1891, the new Mrs. Flesher moved with her husband to a fruit orchard he had leased in the Santa Clara Valley in California. While she awaited the birth of her baby that summer, Helen found many writing assignments to keep her busy. The birth of her first child – a twelve pound boy – ripped her small frame so badly that the doctor had little hope for her recovery. But Helen survived and went back to writing to support her husband while he studied medicine at the University of California. With the reputation built on her Japanese stories, Helen had no difficulty freelancing for local newspapers and magazines across the United States until her husband had completed his medical studies in 1894. By this time, Helen's mother, who had been living with them for some time, bought two small weekly newspapers, and Helen took on the jobs of editor and business manager. Although she had had no experience in either field, within a year she had not only turned the editorial content of both papers into something that would "stimulate women's minds" but also succeeded in making them financially viable.

Unfortunately, this hard-won financial security was short-lived. Helen agreed to sell her newspapers when her husband was offered a post with the famous Doctors Mayo, who were attracting the best talents to their new clinic in Rochester, Minnesota. It was too good an opportunity to turn down, and Helen was convinced that her role was to help her husband and not hold him back in order to cling to their new-found economic security. When this deal fell through, the family settled in Faribault, Minnesota, where Helen returned to free-lancing.

Since her days in California, Helen had become increasingly interested in defending the rights of the poor and underpriviledged and had used many newspaper articles to unearth irregularities in the administration of justice and government. During her first year in Minnesota, she tracked down a case that linked public officials with commercial supplies in an enormous graft. She discovered that each state institution was administered by a board of its own, and under cover of a multiplicity of boards, loose regulations, and lax inspection, superintendents frequently acted as purveyors to their own institutions, adding corruption to impropriety by supplying poor quality and short weight. The inmates were the sufferers, for they got inedible food, caustic soaps, inferior clothes and linens, and defective equipment. When Helen's protests to the authorities were ignored, she took the story to the independent Minneapolis *Journal,* whose crusading founder-publisher was only too pleased to champion a cause that was morally right and uncork "a public stench" as well. The ensuing publicity forced the government to hold an official investigation followed by an administrative shake-up and dismissals.

Helen, however, was not content merely to expose the culprits; she had done that before only to find the same situation cropping up again. Moreover, at thirty-seven, she was experienced enough to realize that exposing corruption would not prevent it from recurring and that the only reliable safeguard was to instigate reform legislation. She decided to lobby for new legislation. Over a year passed, but nothing happened. Her one-woman drive for reform legislation seemed doomed, but even in the face of almost overwhelming opposition and dwindling public support, with only her husband's and mother's encouragement, Helen persisted. At last, her efforts paid off and she was urged to sit on a committee to draft changes. A whole schedule of reforms was drawn up which culminated in the creation of the Minnesota State Board of Control, a tightly regulated body in charge of all state institutions. This was Helen's first public victory in reform legislation and marked the beginning of a new and lasting phase in her life.

In 1901, Helen's husband died suddenly, leaving her with little money and two sons to support. Helen, deciding that a steady job was the only way she could conserve her small capital for emergencies, accepted the position of exchange editor on the *Globe*, and moved the family to St. Paul.

It was during these years in St. Paul that Helen married for the second time. An old beau from her Trinity days, with whom she had corresponded from time to time, decided to pay Helen a visit and in time Helen accepted his offer of marriage. As Jim MacGill, a lawyer and some-time writer for the *Victoria Times* and the *Vancouver Daily Province*, lived in Vancouver, the family faced another move. Helen and her mother, who had been living with her for years, soon adjusted to their new surroundings and became prominent members of the community through their involvement in various women's societies and charitable organizations.

During the next three years, Helen gave birth to two daughters and settled into a period of contented domesticity. But her compulsive energy soon drove her into public life again. She joined the Women's Musical Club, helped form the Vancouver Women's Press Club and became an active member in the Women's University Club of British Columbia – the hub of feminism on the coast. The idea of such a club for college women was highly novel in British Columbia and, since there was as yet no university in the province, it had only a few members. Like Helen, these women were convinced that their advanced education placed them in debt to society, and they felt that a woman had a public duty as well as a private one to her family. Consequently, they had established a special committee to investigate the provincial laws pertaining to women and children. As committee chairman, Helen MacGill discovered that many of the existing laws in the province had been drawn up to meet conditions in England in the 1850's. Among other things, she was appalled to learn that a law in British

Columbia had a provision sanctioning the marriage of children of twelve or fourteen on consent of the father; that a father had sole control of the disposition, management, education and religion of his children, including the unborn child; and that the statute regulating divorce in the province was the English Marriage and Divorce Act of 1856 which firmly established "inequality of cause" between male and female petitioners. When Helen led a delegation to Premier McBride and Attorney-General Bowser in order to get these archaic laws amended she was met with apathy. Despite their promises to give the matter "their earnest consideration," they did nothing. But while session after session of the legislature ended with the offending statutes unamended, Helen and her delegation worked steadily to make the public aware of the situation. By word-of-mouth, correspondence, and press reports, they managed to inform women of their legal status in the province. In sum, Helen said, they aimed to provide a political education for a politically inept class.

Helen had had many opportunities to see just how ignorant women in British Columbia were of their legal rights and had formed some ideas of how to fight the injustices. Through her efforts to bring about reforms in the law, Helen had gained a reputation throughout the city as a champion of the weak and oppressed. Sensing her ready sympathy and concern, people in trouble sought her advice on legal, financial, and domestic problems. One woman's husband, for instance, had sent their two young children back to Ontario for his mother to bring up. In attempting to right the situation, Helen witnessed first hand the cruelty and injustice of a law that gave the woman no legal rights in the matter. Another woman had lost her home to the crown because her husband had died intestate. Helen's husband, Jim, tried to reclaim it for her but in vain because, once again, the law gave women no protection in such situations. And yet another unfortunate woman was left poverty-stricken after her husband had spent all her money and willed his own money elsewhere. Again, Helen could do nothing to help her as during the first decade of the century women in British Columbia had no property rights under the law. Disturbed and angered by the injustices tolerated and even perpetrated by these laws, Helen decided to try to change them.

She became an expert on social law and came to see suffrage as the powerful lever in social reform. In an article for *Liberty Magazine*, she pointed out that the inability of Quebec women to effect change in their antiquated laws was the direct result of their not having a vote:

> Quebec's women may agitate as they please for better Laws; but having no ballot either to tempt or to threaten unheeding representatives they plead in vain. They have not the one thing the politician values – the ballot. They are not the person he respects — the voter.

Helen became an avid supporter of women's suffrage, and quickly learned the best tactics to use with skeptics who wondered "what good it would do for women to have the vote." Like Nellie McClung, Helen saw the need to educate the public about the need for women's suffrage. Enlisting the aid of judges and barristers, she organized lectures on women and the law. For the rest of her life she continued to speak to women's groups advising them on the best strategies to follow, and always offering proposals which were blunt and to the point. At the age of seventy-three, she told a group of Montreal women: "If you women can not change the mind of your Premier, you must change your Premier; even the Bible remonstrates against putting new wine in old bottles!"

During these years Helen also led a fund drive to raise money for a "Women's Building" in Vancouver. When both the Women's Press Club and the University Women's Club found their regular quarters expropriated in 1910 during the building boom in Vancouver, Helen came up with a practical solution. "Why don't we get a building of our own where women's societies can meet and not find themselves suddenly on the street?" As a result, the Vancouver Building Ltd. was formed –

the first organization of its kind in Canada – with Helen as its president and prime organizer. Helen's idea proved highly successful and in time the women launched an all-out campaign for money to build new premises. At last, in May 1926, the Lieutenant-Governor of the province laid the cornerstone for the new Women's Building. At the opening ceremony Helen pledged "to house here the living soul of women's organizations who mother and guard the welfare of children and women, the sad, the sick, the neglected, and dependent."

Helen's long years of work did not go unrecognized. In July 1917, she was appointed Judge of the Juvenile Court of Vancouver, a post she held, except for a brief interval, for twenty-eight years. Her appointment was part of a gradually emerging trend that signalled a dramatic change of attitude in the legal profession. In appointing her to the bench, British Columbia was following the example of Alberta which had appointed Emily Murphy, and later Alice Jamieson, to the Juvenile Court in Edmonton. Since at that time judges did not have to be lawyers, Helen's lack of formal training was no problem. In fact, the press applauded her appointment in view of her "exceptional qualifications, knowledge and elevated judicial mind." There was, however, still the odd anti-feminist voice amid the general praise; there were still some people who were angered at the thought of a woman "doing a man's work," or "being set in judgment over men," or "drawing a salary when she [had] a husband to support her."

Helen approached her work as a judge with characteristic vigour and integrity. To begin with, she found the penal system in British Columbia in 1916 was very much in need of reform. Probation was seldom used; in fact, there were no female probation officers. The detention home, the court's "lock-up," had no school and no teacher. And the industrial schools, the court's "reformatories," gave no training and no rehabilitation. Helen was appalled at these conditions and declared that the "so-called Juvenile Court which operates as a petty Police

Court betrays us...The community is betrayed and the offenders wronged in that nothing better is shown or taught, and the culprits are not helped to better things."

Helen's criticism of the courts and reformatories was based on her belief that, whereas "the Police Court [may work] to put adult offenders in gaol, the Court [should work] to keep child offenders out of gaol." With this as her guideline, the new judge set about improving the system. Among other things, she worked to establish basic services to help children from reformatories re-establish themselves in society; she stressed the importance of probation as a safeguard against future temptations; she brought in teachers to the detention home; and she restructured detention schools for girls to include job-training. Throughout her career as judge, she wrote many articles and pamphlets dealing with legislation, juvenile delinquency, and child labour, and gave lectures throughout the province.

While she struggled with the expected resistance to change, Helen's problems were compounded by the usual prejudice against her sex, which took the form of petty harrassments and wrangling over regulations; the streetcar pass, the invitations, the use of an official car, and other routine privileges attached to her job were withheld or delayed for Judge MacGill. Annoying and frustrating as such tactics were, Helen refused to waste time or energy on annoying but inconsequential squabbles with small-minded bureaucrats. Moreover, she recognized that, in her role as one of the few women judges, she was fighting a battle for all groups that were discriminated against to gain access to positions of prestige and power. Because of this, she was careful not to jeopardize their chances by creating unnecessary ill-will.

As might be expected, anyone as active in reform work as Helen had her share of enemies and disappointments. The most upsetting to Helen was the unexpected loss of her appointment after the defeat of the Liberals whom the MacGills had supported for years. Jim, always an ardent Liberal, had convinced his wife that she would get no justice from the Tories, who, he said, "were solidly aligned against the political rights of her sex." And so it was that her politics and not her sex cost her the job. When the Liberals were defeated in the provincial election of 1928, the new Tory Attorney-General re-issued the appointments of all Vancouver magistrates and judges of the Juvenile Court – except one. Helen alone was not reappointed, and her former job was given to another woman – a Tory and a defeated candidate in the recent election.

The move, although devised to get rid of Helen, was entirely legal for, on January 1, 1929, South Vancouver, Point Grey, and the city proper merged to form Greater Vancouver, an event that allowed the Attorney-General to rescind the appointments of all the Vancouver magistrates and judges of the Juvenile Court and re-issue them for the new jurisdiction. The move caused a furor in the press and among women's groups: "The Juvenile Court – Political Jugglery" ran the headline in the *Daily Province*, a Conservative paper; "Judge MacGill's Dismissal – the Spoils System," accused the independent *Star*. Within days, Helen had become the object of a *cause célèbre*, and a group of women in the Maritimes organized the Judge MacGill Reinstatement Committee. The champion of so many public causes was troubled and uncertain when her own interests were at stake. "If it were anyone but myself, I would know what to do," she told her husband who, for the sake of dignity, urged her to remain aloof.

With time, however, public interest in Helen's dismissal waned, and Helen was left to go on with her life as best she could. She continued to serve on numerous organizations and to act as an unofficial consultant on problems regarding juveniles. It was not until 1934, after the Liberals were swept back into power under a new leader, that Helen was re-appointed Justice of the Peace and Judge of the Juvenile Court of Greater Vancouver. Once again, she decried the archaic correctional methods that overlooked "the paramount good of the child" and announced the ground-rules that would lead to reform: "The reformatories should be used only as a last resort!" "Probation is the key-stone of the arch of juvenile reclamation!" As one official said, it was as if Helen had never been away.

Aging proved difficult for Helen. At fifty, she began to look "a bit eccentric"; her petite figure had filled out and she was severely handicapped by rapidly deteriorating eyesight which threatened to leave her blind. Never one with much clothes sense, and because of her poor vision and spasmodic lack of money over the years, she had often tended to look shabby. As she grew older, she paid even less attention to her appearance and buried herself more and more in her work which she had come to approach with an intensity bordering on fanaticism. At seventy-three, although well past the retirement age for most people, she clung to her job and became secretive about her age. Refusing to give in to the infirmities of growing old, she set herself the same rigorous schedule she had followed when she was much younger. Besides her work, she continued to write articles, give lectures, and attend conferences. In 1936, she attended the first Canadian Penal Conference where she was quoted for such practical views as: "The test of a prison is the number of prisoners who never return." There were tributes, too, in recognition of her years of public service and her dedication to improving laws for women and children. In 1938, Helen wrote an enthusiastic letter to her children informing them that the Senate of the University of British Columbia had unanimously resolved to offer her a Doctor of Laws degree, Honoris Causa. One of the few women to be so honoured at that time, Helen was delighted and joked with her children that she was not just getting "one of those old Ph.D.'s...but a genuine honest-to-goodness LLd. (sic)."

Jim's sudden death in 1939 caused Helen to retreat into her work more than ever. Although her children wrote often and visited from time to time, for the most part Helen lived alone carrying on with her writing, public speaking and court duties.

When she was seventy-nine, she told a group of young business-men: "All who engage in Juvenile Court work realize that yes-terday's neglected child is today's juvenile delinquent and to-morrow's criminal." Nor did age rob her of her whimsical view of life and unpretentious humour. Once when a huge police-man ushered a tiny child into court, she remarked: "That's pretty small fry, Constable. When you catch a little fish like that, don't you usually throw it back again?"

At the age of eighty-two, Helen was terrified by the prospect of retirement and a life of enforced idleness. Her son's sudden death in 1944 helped to precipitate a coronary occlusion and, unable to live alone, she moved to Toronto where she spent the last two years of her life with her youngest daughter. Even then, weak, unsteady, and all but blind, Helen could not resign her-self to idleness. Driven to do something each day, she would go to her daughter's office and spend the day lying on a sofa talk-ing of her plans. When she became stronger, she tried to finish a study on juvenile reclamation, a few chapters of which had already been published, but she never completed it.

Helen MacGill died in 1947 while visiting her other daughter in Chicago, ending a life that, among many successes, had accomplished at least one triumph; it gave a final, elo-quent, and definitive answer to one of the current questions of her day, "Why give a university training to a girl?"

Nellie McClung (1874-1951).

CHAPTER SIX

Writers for Reform

Ever since pioneer days, Canadian women have turned to writing as a means of coping with the frustrations in their lives. Even a cursory glance at some of these recently published letters and diaries – such as those of Sophia McNab, Julia Lambert, and Anna Leveridge – reveals the mental as well as the physical hardships these women endured in their efforts to forge a new life in a difficult and hostile environment. With a few exceptions, like Susannah Moodie and Catherine Parr Traill, relatively few of these writers intended to publish their impressions. In the 1890's, however, two factors – a growing market for Canadian books and the emergence of a new social consciousness – encouraged women to write for an audience and to use their writing as a vehicle for social criticism. Looking back at these factors, one can see that both stemmed, in part, from Canada's population explosion at the turn of the century. In the decade from 1901 to 1911 alone, close to two million settlers of all nationalities poured into the country, well over a million of whom chose to live in the West. Their arrival rekindled the dreams of prosperity that Canadians had once held for the vast and empty western Prairies – dreams that most people had abandoned during the long depression that lasted from the mid-1870's to the mid 1890's. This sudden burst of prosperity produced in its wake a wave of nationalism. "The whole country seemed to be outward bound, conscious of its emerging identity, and conscious also of its ability to speak for itself," explained Lorne Pierce of Ryerson Press. "We were at the beginning of things as a nation." As a result of these trends, for at least a decade Canadians were eagerly searching for new reading material on their country. Publishers were quick to exploit the new demand for books; in fact, a dozen new publishing houses were established in Toronto between 1896 and 1911.

In addition to this sudden prosperity, Canada's rapid population growth spawned a series of social ills that were particularly evident in urban areas where slum living and bad working conditions exacerbated the other problems confronting immigrants. Not only did their private dreams for a better life crumble in the "promised land," they also lost the most stabilizing elements of their former existences – the traditional values of family, religion, and culture. Robbed of these guidelines, they struggled to adjust to the grim and unexpected realities of life amid poverty, prejudice, and disease. In an effort to relieve their despair or find expression for their bitterness, some turned to drink or crime. In her autobiography *Confessions of an Immigrant's Daughter*, Laura Salverson wrote "every beautiful thing [I saw] intensified my resentment against the cruel inequalities of life...it was not that I coveted any of these domestic trappings ...It was the atmosphere these things created, the sense of security and well-being that made gracious living a matter of course."

Traditional institutions seemed incapable of coping with these sudden social ills. Anglican, Presbyterian, and Methodist Churches, for instance, failed to adjust their thinking to accommodate such realistic facts of daily existence as the oppressive and crippling effects of poverty. The new reform movement produced by these inadequacies prompted the whole of society to self-examination. This new social consciousness was not uniquely Canadian; it was part of a widespread attempt in Europe and North America to revive and develop Christian social insights and to apply them to the emerging forms of a collective society.

Based partly on a belief that women possessed a higher moral sense than men, a form of feminism developed that aimed to harness this morality and apply it to the good of society in general. However, when reform-minded women tried to institute social changes, they discovered that they had little hope of making any progress without the effective power of the vote and that they had little hope of gaining that necessary weapon without the support of other women. Consequently, they organized suffrage groups dedicated to the sole purpose of educating the public about the need for and the value to be gained from women's suffrage.

As might be expected in this climate, much of the writing of the time was permeated with national pride, social awareness, and women's suffrage. Writers from immigrant backgrounds, like Laura Salverson, used writing not only as a means of coming to terms with the frustrations they experienced while watching their parents trying to adjust to a new culture in a strange land, but also to show that immigrants, too, had aspirations beyond the physical jobs most of them occupied. "I longed to justify my race as more than hewers of wood," Mrs. Salverson wrote about her work. In her autobiography, published in 1939, and in several of her highly romantic novels, Mrs. Salverson (1880-1970) mirrors the story of countless twentieth-century immigrants in the developing West: she tells of the westward migration in search of fortune, the disillusionment between settlers' expectations and the reality they confronted, the illness and death, the yearly arrival of babies too feeble to live, and the constant and enervating struggle against the forces of poverty.

Another socially conscious writer, Emily Murphy (better known before her crusades for women's rights as Janey Canuck) came West during this high tide of immigration and poured her dreams for Canada's great future into her three books of sketches about life around her. Seeing herself as one of the builders of a new and magic land, she used her writing to help set things "good and true." *Janey Canuck in the West, Open Trails,* and *Seeds of Pine,* reflect her attempt to shape her cherished vision of the future of the West, which she saw as invigorating and regenerating – a land where there was no need of "the ologies and osophies, the big causes, cultures and cants" that had been the props of her former "canned life" in the East. With the pride of a doting parent, Emily sang the praises of the West's progressive, free spirit. But always mindful of the future, she was quick to point out the faults, like the public discriminatory attitude towards the Doukhobors. She branded their critics as unfriendly, jealous, misguided, and ignorant, gave examples to show that their prejudice was born of rumour not fact, and led her readers to conclude that the Doukhobors had "a saner, nobler, and more natural ideal for existence than their critics."

While the "Janey Canuck" books are all stamped with their author's nationalism, Nellie McClung's books can be seen as vehicles for the feminism of her era. She used her writing to show what she described as "the pitiful plight of woman in a world as made by man." Nellie wasn't exaggerating either, for although some women in a few areas had been granted the right to vote in municipal elections in the nineteenth century, no Canadian woman had the right to vote in federal elections until 1917, and no Canadian woman could vote in provincial elections until 1916 when one by one the western provinces granted woman's suffrage.

It is difficult to estimate the influence these writers-cum-social-reformers exerted on public opinion, especially since most spoke from many platforms – as authors, public speakers, and political activists. When one looks at the popularity of their books, the importance of books in the lives of Canadians at the time, and the correlation between their books and certain social development such as women's suffrage, one can sense the deluge of ideas these women managed to inject into the often resistant veins of public opinion in the quick and easy-to-take serum of their very popular books. Considering the large circulation their books enjoyed in their day, one must assume that their ideas reached and struck a responsive chord in the public. For instance, at the time when 4,000 copies was considered a good sale in Canada, *Sowing Seeds in Danny* by Nellie McClung sold over 100,000 copies and ran to seventeen editions; its sequel, *The Second Chance,* published in 1901, was even more successful. Emily Murphy's books were also bestsellers: *Open Trails* (1912) sold over 60,000 copies, and both this book and *Janey Canuck in the West* (1910) sold enough copies to warrant being reprinted by Dent in the Wayfarer's Library.

Fiction, especially those works that relied heavily on melodrama and social comment, was very popular at the beginning of the century. These Canadian writers were following earlier American and British models whose prime purpose was to instruct by entertaining and by engaging the reader emotionally. In addition to the popularity of their style and form, not to mention the growing interest in reading, the social content of these writers' books must have added to their appeal at a time when social issues were very much in vogue. For instance, Nellie McClung's most dogmatic feminist tract, *In Times Like These,* appeared in 1915, the year before women were granted provincial suffrage in Manitoba, Saskatchewan, and Alberta. Laura Salverson's *The Viking Heart,* published in 1923, can also be seen as an attempt to give a tender and sympathetic portrayal of the lot of immigrants.

Despite their popularity and appeal, it is difficult to estimate the effect of these women's writing on the political and social events of the time. But whatever their direct results, their works do seem to have fulfilled Nellie McClung's aim, which was to act "like a leaven upon the solid mass of public opinion." In her autobiography, *The Stream Runs Fast,* Nellie McClung seems to be speaking for all of them when she acknowledged the belief in the power of ideas. "It was not ideas I was giving them exactly but rather ferments – something which I hoped would work like yeast in their minds...Ideas are epidemic – they go like measles."

Nellie McClung

Nellie McClung's sense of social injustice was long in the making. As a young teacher on the Prairies in the 1890's she had been shocked at farm women's unbearably hard lives and had dreamed of helping them to remove the heavy yoke of tradition which Nellie saw as responsible for their continuing acceptance of misery. She could never forget those farm women whose lives in the days before electricity, running water, and other labour-saving devices, revolved around a never-ending and physically exhausting routine of child-bearing, housework, and farm work. The farmyards of the time were filled with equipment to lighten men's work-load, but in the kitchens nothing had changed – or was likely to change.

Many women who could not bear the strain, retired almost gratefully to an early grave. Nellie remembered reading of the death of a farmer's wife, aged thirty-three, who left six small children to mourn her loss. The obituary closed piously with the words: "Thy will be done." Although puritanism was deeply entrenched in the Prairies and its constraints had no doubt helped pioneers endure many hardships, the Christian resignation it preached now seemed to Nellie to be keeping women from progressing. "I did not believe that it was the will of God that had taken away this young mother," she said defiantly. In fact, the general complacency at the high mortality rate in young women amazed her, but, she noted, "their places were filled without undue delay, [as] soon as some man's sister or sister-in-law came from Ontario to take the dead woman's place." Nellie could not blame women for giving up when life offered not even the hope for better days. Sometimes those who lived seemed more like pale husks of womanhood anyway.

The mother of one of her students was married to a drunkard and annually produced a baby she neither wanted nor could afford. What happiness had she ever had? What had she to look forward to but more of the same? Such women did not even have the time to enjoy their children Nellie realized one day after reading a letter from the mother of another of her students. "Dear Miss Mooney," wrote Mrs. Burns, "I wish you would cut Jimmy's hair. He looks like the colts do in spring, but I can't get it done, and I guess you won't mind; for you have more time than I have."

Nellie also realized that the gross disparities between the sexes in legal, economic, and social areas meant that these women had nothing to show for their efforts. The pitiful plight of a sixty-five year old woman who was provided for in her husband's will only to the extent that she was to keep her youngest son, made Nellie conscious of the fact that women had few more legal rights than animals. In another case, a widow was living in an isolated cabin under an assumed name in order to prevent her influential father-in-law from claiming his grandson, an inhuman act which under the existing laws concerning guardianship he had every right to do since his son, the child's father, had died.

As Nellie went from one teaching post to another in the next five years, she realized that much of women's suffering was needless. But she knew that despite the injustices inflicted upon them most women were inclined to suffer in silence. Witness the wife of the town drunkard, she thought. Nellie felt a sort of pity for her but it was also mixed with contempt for "she was such a door-mat; [and] even washed for the hotel-keeper's wife to pay old Silas' liquor bills."

Nellie's thoughts were crystallized by an incident at a quilting bee she attended in town one Saturday in 1890. All was going well until word came that the local minister's wife, Mrs. McClung, was coming by to get signatures on a petition asking that women be granted the vote. The quilters hurried upstairs rather than face a confrontation, leaving only Nellie and the hostess to handle the situation. The latter sat uneasily on the edge of her chair obviously hoping that the minister's wife wouldn't come. "Those interfering Methodists," she had just finished saying when the troublemaker appeared.

At that time, women had neither the municipal, provincial, or federal vote, and the mere mention of the word "suffrage" produced violent reactions in many quarters. Although women's suffrage was a new subject to the sixteen-year-old Nellie, she signed the petition out of admiration for Mrs. McClung. Only after the troublemaker had left with her one signature did the women again descend, eager to vent their anger against those who dared challenge the status quo.

"It's an insult to our husbands even to ask for the vote," said one woman whom Nellie recognized as the wife of the town drunkard. Nellie was surprised to see how bitter these church women were. She could see that even the teacher friend who had brought her to the quilting bee was now looking at her scornfully, and yet this same teacher was as appalled as she was at the many injustices to women in the area. "I wanted to tell them about how the minister's wife had come into the Wheeler's house, taken charge and delivered the poor woman's baby when her husband had failed to stay off the bottle long enough to get the doctor...I know women should help each other and I could see that the vote would bring an added importance to women...but I could not put it into words. They had me down." Nonetheless, Nellie refused to change her views and apologize for supporting women's suffrage.

From their first meeting, Nellie had been impressed by Mrs. McClung, the woman who, although neither of them knew it then, was to exert a large influence on Nellie's life. When they first met, Nellie was only sixteen, fresh from normal school in Winnipeg where she had taken the five months' course.

Apart from this brief period in Winnipeg and her early years in Ontario which she hardly remembered, her view of the outside world had been limited to those glimpses provided by articles and stories in the weekly edition of the *Family Herald* from Montreal. Because there was no school in the area until she was ten, Nellie was a late-starter in school and, partly as a result of this, all her life was driven by a passion to learn. Mrs. McClung shared the same passion and, as Nellie described her, she had "all the sweetness, charm and beauty of the old-fashioned woman...[and] in addition to this, she had a fearless, and even radical mind." Influenced by Mrs. McClung's interest in politics, Nellie attended her first political meeting, where she and her friend were the only women present. All went well until Nellie asked the candidate his party's views on extending the vote to women. He laughed, looked down at them with a paternal rebuke in his eyes, then ignored them for the rest of the evening. Riding home that night, side-saddle as custom demanded, Nellie was thrown. Picking herself up she angrily denounced the senseless custom: "If I had been riding the right and natural way, astride the horse, this could not have happened...a sidesaddle is surely the last word in discomfort for both the rider and the horse and another example of life's injustice to women."

Gradually, Nellie was forming the basis of the feminist philosophy that was to permeate all her writing. At the same time, she had fallen in love with Wes McClung, the son of her great friend. Wes was away studying to become a pharmacist but the couple wrote and planned to marry when he had established himself. And so, in August 1896, Nellie began a new life as housewife in the young couple's apartment above Wes' pharmacy in Manitou.

Although she had given up her job (at the time school boards did not employ married women teachers), Nellie was kept busy running her apartment, writing sketches in her diary, and preparing for the birth of her first child. This latter experience made her even more adamant that women should work to change things and not merely endure them. Faced with daily bouts of morning sickness she questioned her husband as to why something had not been found to save women from this nausea. "If it had been a man's disease," she decided, "it would have been made the subject of scientific research and relieved long ago. But women could suffer; it kept them humble!" By now, Nellie had concluded that women's resignation to their lot was born of years of suffering which had snuffed out their hopes for a better life. Not content to join in such apathy, she decided to do something to change things.

> I wanted to write, to do for the people around me what Dickens had done for his people. I wanted to be a voice for the voiceless as he had been a defender of the weak, a flaming fire that would consume the dross that encrusts human souls, a spring of sweet water beating up through all this bitter world to refresh and nourish souls that were ready to faint.

Despite her youthful vows to change things, between giving birth to and raising five children, Nellie had little time for anything else. She became so wrapped up in her role as housewife, that her mother-in-law had to force her to write the story that ultimately launched her on her literary career.

"Colliers has a short story contest particularly for unknown writers," she greeted Nellie one morning, "and I think you should send in one. You can write and...it seems like a great chance." When Nellie objected that she hadn't the time, her mother-in-law replied, "Don't you know that conditions are never perfect? Life conspires to keep a woman tangled in trifles ...Alice and I are in charge so you are free." Nellie went upstairs and wrote the story that would eventually form the basis of her first novel, *Sowing Seeds in Danny*. Although she didn't win a prize, she did receive an encouraging letter complimenting her on her writing ability. Spurred on by this praise, Nellie sent her story to a friend in the literary field and he, in turn, showed it to a publisher.

Three years went by, and she had almost forgotten it. Then a letter arrived to rekindle her hopes. Quickly tearing it open, she read with mounting excitement that E.S. Caswell, editor at Wm. Briggs Publishing Co. in Toronto, had found her manuscript in a forgotten file, read it, and been impressed by its vitality, humour, and originality. He encouraged her to make it into a book.

Driven by her renewed enthusiasm, Nellie plunged ahead

and within a year had completed *Sowing Seeds in Danny* which, after more delays with the publishers, finally appeared in 1908.

Unselfishly, Nellie attributed not only her start in writing but also her start in public speaking to her mother-in-law. She was at first reluctant when Mrs. McClung asked her to read a chapter from *Sowing Seeds in Danny* to help raise money for the w.c.t.u.'s (Women's Christian Temperance Union) new home for friendless girls in Winnipeg, but in the end she agreed. Despite her fears that her first appearance was a failure, Nellie soon began to receive invitations to speak. In a few years, in fact, she became one of Manitoba's most popular public speakers addressing over 400 public meetings between 1913 and 1921 and delighting audiences with her common touch and no-nonsense approach to life.

Part of Nellie's popularity as a speaker stemmed from her notoriety for, by this time, in addition to being an author of some note, she was also well known as one of the foremost feminists in the West. This was partly the result of circumstances, for, when Wes McClung sold his pharmacy in 1911 to go into the insurance business and moved the family to Winnipeg, Nellie found herself immersed in a strong current of feminism. As a member of the Local Council of Women she soon became involved in a difficult struggle to change the dreadful working conditions for women in factories. Many workers, it seemed, were afraid to confront management for fear of losing their jobs, and some members of the Local Council were afraid to get involved with anything that might reflect adversely on their husbands. Scorning such selfish caution, Nellie refused to be dissuaded from her mission and, together with another woman, invited the provincial premier, Sir Rodmond Roblin, to tour some factories. Nellie concludes that her friend must have had political connections because the pompous premier accepted and, flanked by his two attractive guides, set out with the confidence and complacency that comes from being firmly seated on a political throne. At the outset he told them that he believed in work for young woman, since there was too much idleness, especially with electricity and short-cuts in labour. He warned Nellie and her friend not to get too upset about women's working conditons. "Mind you, he liked kind women and hoped they would never change, but these girls whom Nellie thought were underpaid, they probably worked only because they wanted pin-money. Anyway, working wouldn't hurt them, it would keep them off the streets." Knowing what lay ahead, Nellie and her friend listened politely. When they led their guest, then in his early sixties, down dark, slippery stairs to an airless basement, they noticed his manner had changed. The light in the basement workroom came from gaunt light bulbs, hanging from the ceiling. The floor was littered with refuse and there was no ventilation and no heat. Nellie urged him to talk to some of the workers but he refused. Not about to let him escape so easily though, the two women took him into a foul passage where a queue had formed before a door marked "toilet." "For God's sake, let me out of here. I'm choking! I never knew such a hell-hole existed!" Sir Rodmond exclaimed. On the way home he gave Nellie a perplexed look and commented: "I still can't see why two women like you should ferret out such utterly disgusting things." Obviously he was as much upset about them as he had been by what he had just seen. Nonetheless, he promised to look into the matter and, with this understanding the women said goodbye.

Changes, however, were not forthcoming and these reform-minded women realized once again that they needed the powerful lever of the vote if they were ever to succeed in bringing about social reforms. As a result, in 1912 Nellie and some fifteen avowed suffragettes formed the Political Equality League dedicated to the sole purpose of winning the provincial vote for women. The committee aimed to train public speakers with a view to arousing public sentiment on the issue of women's suffrage. As might be expected, the ebullient Nellie was an intrepid rabble-rouser. One day, on an impulse, she phoned the Premier's office and asked for an interview. To her surprise, she was invited to come over right away.

"What in the world do women want to vote for? Why do women want to mix in the hurly-burly of politics?" he asked after listening to Nellie's plea for women's suffrage. "Nice women don't want the vote."

"That's all very nice to hear," Nellie said unabashedly, "but unfortunately that's not enough. The women of Manitoba believe that the time has come to make an effort to obtain political equality. The laws are very unfair to women. I would like to tell you about some of them, for I don't believe you know." Sir Rodmond balked, however, and said the Cabinet wouldn't listen to her. "You'd be surprised," she argued defiantly. "I'm really not too hard to listen to, and I don't believe the Cabinet would mind...it would be a welcome change in the middle of a dull day."

At this the Premier lost all patience: "I think you're rather a conceited young woman, who has perhaps had some success at Friday afternoon entertainments at country school houses, and so are labouring under the delusion that you have the gift of oratory." They were at opposite poles, so Nellie left, more determined than ever to fight for women's suffrage.

In the next few years she devoted herself to writing pamphlets for the League and distributing evidence on the status of women in the province. When the League borrowed the idea of a mock parliament that suffragettes in Ontario had used so successfully before the turn of the century, Nellie played a key role. In their version, suffragettes took the parts of members of the Cabinet, and the men came begging for rights for men only to be rudely brushed aside by the woman premier. Nellie played the role of the man who had become her prime adversary, the complacent, anti-feminist Premier Roblin, and burlesqued his manner so realistically that she left the packed Walker Theatre in Winnipeg rocking with laughter but also aware of the need for women's suffrage.

Suffragettes of Nellie's day based their arguments for equal rights on two seemingly contradictory premises: the one, that women were more moral than men, and the other, that they were equal to men. Evidently this paradox bothers modern day feminists more than it did their forerunners who never tried to resolve it. Certainly, it didn't bother reporters covering the mock parliament. Even the pro-government *Telegram* reported that "Mrs. McClung's reply to the appeal for 'votes for men' was the choicest piece of sarcasm ever heard locally." More important from a practical point of view, the League raised enough money from their efforts to campaign for the Liberals who supported women's franchise in the election in 1915. Although the Conservatives were returned to power, their majority was substantially decreased, and they were defeated in the house a year later over a government scandal. With the party they had supported in power, suffragettes in Manitoba were hopeful but nonetheless continued their propaganda campaign.

The task of uprooting old ideas and of propagating new ones had not only proved frustrating and time-consuming but also produced in its wake a bevy of enemies for all members of the League. As its volatile spokesman as well as being a celebrated author, Nellie McClung became the choice target for much of the abuse. Her antagonists heckled her on every wicket, belittling her powers of oratory, criticizing her for failing in her duties as wife and deriding her for neglecting her children. According to Nellie, during the big political fight over women's suffrage in 1913, the *Telegram* in Winnipeg was running cartoons of her every day and often depicted her children as unfortunate, ragged offspring left alone to manage while their mother stormed the bastions of the Legislature. Nellie took it all with charactristic aplomb and never changed her course. "Never retract, never explain, never apologize – get the thing done and let them howl" was her motto.

Sometimes, Nellie repeated critics' stories, such as one by a local woman reporter who wrote a column explaining why she would always be able to tell Alberta women when she went to Heaven: "They will be there in little groups with pencil and notebooks, by the side of the river of life, giving the finishing touches to resolution B.72894, urging that more rural children be taken into the Heavenly Choirs."

Even Nellie's family learned to cope with public criticism. Nellie amused audiences with the story about the time her three-year-old son ran away. "We were alarmed over his disappearance but before we had time to be greatly disturbed his brother aged eight delivered him at the back door, breathless with joy at being safe home with the young deserter. 'I got him, Mother,' he shouted, 'it's all right, the *Telegram* didn't see him. I sneaked him up the lanes.' "

Despite her audience's laughter and despite what she told them to the contrary, Nellie could not stop attacks on her family. "That is the part of my public life that has really hurt," she said. To those who accused her of neglecting her children and husband, she replied:

> The decree is that [a woman] must stay at home or at least do nothing serious. No one has much to say about the woman that stays away from home for frivolous purposes. I believe I have spent more hours in my own home than the average woman, for I do not play bridge, I am not an habitual attender of teas or dances, and I rarely go out in the evening.

Ironically, in view of the opposition suffragettes confronted, they were not advocating a radical departure from women's traditional role in society. Almost unanimously, they saw motherhood as the highest achievement of their sex, believing as Nellie put it, that "every normal woman desires children." Moreover, they also agreed that a woman's primary role was that of wife and mother, and they saw her public duty to society as an extension of this. In an effort to counteract the public's narrow-mindedness, Nellie tried to point out the value of women working at something besides housework. As far as Nellie was concerned such a woman helped to create a better home environment for all members of the family. Certainly, according to all reports "the McClung home [was] the happiest place in the world." Moreover, Nellie's four sons and one daughter were proud of her efforts and the gains she had helped make, especially when the new Liberal government of Manitoba set a precedent in Canada by granting the provincial franchise to women in January of 1916 – two years to the day since the Local Council of Women's mock parliament.

Unfortunately, Nellie wouldn't be there to witness this long-awaited and hard-won victory: her husband's insurance firm had moved him to Edmonton where she was already immersed in another struggle for women's suffrage. On February 26, 1915, Nellie headed one of the largest delegations that have ever assembled on the floor of the Alberta Legislature to lay before the members of the House the Equal Suffrage petition. This time, however, Nellie's forthright tone had an added note of optimism, since she felt that women's suffrage was in the tide and that it was only a matter of time before it reached women in Alberta. Nor were liberal-minded Albertans about to raise ideological barriers against change. As Nellie put it: "Always in Alberta there is a fresh wind blowing." Consequently, throughout the prairie campaign, women suffragettes received staunch support from their men with no delegation petitioning for women's suffrage appearing without a substantial representation of men. Significantly, this progressiveness in the Canadian prairie provinces concerning women's suffrage had parallels in the United States where pioneer communities were invariably the first to enfranchise women. In the *Woman Suffrage Movement in Canada*, Catherine Cleverdon points out: "On both sides of the border the feeling generally prevailed that women as well as men had opened up the country, had shared the experiences of settling a new land, and were therefore entitled to a voice in making the laws." As might be expected in view of these attitudes and trends, in July 1916, women in Alberta were granted the right to vote in provincial elections. Nellie McClung rejoiced along with other suffragettes but unlike those who lapsed into apathy after they achieved their goal, she looked for new fields, and began urging women to become involved in life outside their homes.

In 1921, Nellie ran for the Legislative Assembly and won – one of five Liberals elected when the United Farmers of Alberta swept away the Liberal government. For the next years, she devoted herself to being a politician, a role she enjoyed although she admitted she was not a good party woman. Her reactions, of course, were totally in character and indicative of many feminists' dislike of party politics.

> I could not vote against some of the government measures which seemed to be right and proper, and I tried to persuade my fellow members that this was the right course to pursue. I believed that we were the executive of the people and should bring our best judgement to bear on every question, irrespective of party ties.

Likewise, when Martha Black was elected M.P. for the Yukon in 1940 as an Independent Conservative, she frequently urged the House not to waste time on partisan politics. And one reason Thérèse Casgrain failed to win support from the federal party in her campaign in 1942 was that she refused to subscribe to Liberal party policy on conscription. Certainly Nellie's views on women's rights did not contribute much to her popularity either in the party or among her constituents. Always outspoken, she advocated mothers' allowances, public health nursing services, free medical and dental care for school children, and new laws on women's property rights. And her campaign for the retention of prohibition eventually ended her political career. Nellie realized that her stand was unpopular. Two days before the election, in fact, an official of the Hotel-keepers' Association came to persuade her to "soft-pedal" her antagonism to the liquor business. Nellie explained that,

> My quarrel has never been with the hotel people...The evil is in the stuff itself, no matter who handles it. Alcohol no doubt has a place in medicine but as a beverage it is a racial poison. It lowers a man's standard of conduct and makes the user pay a heavy price. Every one of you hotel men could run your houses without it, and make money too. Someday humanity will outlaw it just as slavery was wiped out. That took a long time and this will too, but I can't promise that I will ever "lay-off."

Nellie's relentless opposition to alcohol dated from her experiences on the prairie where she had seen women suffer because of drunken husbands. She never forgot their sad stories and filled her novels and short stories with examples of degenerative effects of alcohol. In her very first novel, *Sowing Seeds in Danny*, a boy's drunkenness nearly results in another man's death. Nellie maintained her stand on prohibition despite political and social pressures, and, as a result, she was defeated – although only by sixty votes.

She reacted with her typical honesty to her sudden change of fortunes. A few days later she wrote an article on "How it feels to be a defeated candidate" in which she confessed to venting her frustrations in a regular binge of cooking.

Losing had its compensations. She was glad to be free from some aspects of her former life as an M.L.A. Among other things, she loathed the type of personal inquisition she had been subjected to just because she was a woman in a predominantly male field, and she was relieved not to have to commute from Edmonton to Calgary where her husband had been moved while she was still in office. Now, she could devote herself once again to writing. In the next few years, she published two more books of short stories and essays. She also brought out two volumes of her autobiography: *Clearing in the West* (1935) and *The Stream Runs Fast* (1945) in which she related many incidents which helped form her philosophy of life. In addition, she wrote a weekly column for a paper and continued to contribute stories to various magazines from time to time.

Although she never ran for public office again, Nellie maintained her interest in human rights until her death in 1951. In 1929, she was one of the "five women from Alberta" who, led by Emily Murphy, signed the petition to have women legally declared persons. She was the only Canadian woman appointed to the Canadian War Conference in 1918, the only female voice at the Methodist Ecumenical Congress in 1921, one of the first women appointed to the C.B.C. board of governors in 1930, and a representative on the Canadian delegation to the League of Nations in 1938.

The outbreak of the Second World War in 1939, however, collapsed her hopes for this experiment in world cooperation and shattered her view that women's suffrage would exert a regenerative force on the moral life of the country. The female vote had not only failed to stamp out drunkenness, it failed to end wars. Nellie's disappointment was born of the gap between her idealism and reality, as she realized only too well.

Women could have sobered this country if they had willed it so; that is a sore and withering thought...how could we be so indifferent to the evils which mar our creation. But these bitter observations had no part in our thoughts while we were waging the battle for what we called the emancipation of women. We were so sure that better home conditions, the extension of education and equality of opportunity would develop a happy race of people who would not be dependent on spurious pleasures...We believed that with all our hearts as we went singing up the hill.

Nonetheless, as she gazed at this unexpected unfolding of events and attitudes, Nellie surged with a sense of accomplishment in Canadian women's new and expanding role in society. Like her great friend and ally, Emily Murphy, Nellie took pride in her personal contribution to society.

"In Canada we are developing a pattern of life and I know something about one block of that pattern," she said, "I know it, for I helped to make it."

Clara Brett Martin (1874-1923).

Emily Howard Stowe (1831-1903).

Maude Abbott (1869-1940).

Cora Hind (1861-1942).

CHAPTER SEVEN

The Professions —
No Room at the Top

A few women began to infiltrate male-dominated professions in Canada in the latter half of the nineteenth century, but by stepping outside the traditional boundaries established for their sex they invoked criticism and protest from all classes of society. Such outbursts of anti-feminism and prejudice created many difficulties for these women and deterred some of them from pursuing careers in their chosen fields. Louise McKinney, for example, one of Canada's most active members of the Women's Christian Temperance Union and a noted suffragette, dreamed of becoming a doctor only to discover that few medical schools in Canada accepted women in the 1880's. Although she altered her plans and trained as a teacher instead, her disappointment was a contributing factor in her life-long crusade for women's rights. A few women, whether through a selfish wish for a career, a desire to break down sexist barriers, or for basic economic reasons, persevered with their respective goals and, wittingly or not, gradually helped to change women's role in society.

Although these women were in different fields and in different parts of the country, their desire to escape the narrow confines of their allotted role in nineteenth-century society reflected a growing undercurrent among Canadian women at that time. Their rejection of the traditional role was the inevitable result of many women's veiled discontent with their life which had been simmering unnoticed for years. "Oh, how I longed to preach salvation to a dying world, and tell of the redeeming grace and undying love," wrote Mary Bradley from New Brunswick, who longed to be a preacher, a calling denied to women. She drew strength from the fervent hope that "at some future day, God by his Providence, would open a door and put [her] on the way to be useful."

Needless to say, this new awakening was not an isolated phenomenon, but drew inspiration from progressive movements elsewhere in the world. Whereas in Canada the first woman did not graduate from medical school until 1883, Elizabeth Blackwell graduated from Geneva Medical College, New York, in 1849. By the time Clara Brett Martin applied to study law in Toronto in 1897, the United States was admitting women to study and practise law and had, in fact, more women lawyers than the whole of Europe. As we have seen, the Toronto *Globe* editors were skeptical about publishing Helen MacGill's stories on the West, but an American magazine, *Cosmopolitan*, hired her as a correspondent to cover the opening of the first Japanese Diet in Tokyo in December 1890. Despite these promising stirrings at home and abroad, there was a general opposition to change of any kind in Canada. This was particularly evident to newcomers who, accustomed to more liberal ideas elsewhere, found many Canadian customs, attitudes, and laws archaic. When Alice Ravenhill emigrated in 1911, for example, she was appalled at the conservatism she found in Canada. In her *Memoirs*, Miss Ravenhill, a noted English authority on public health, observed that

Active participation of women in public affairs, social, philanthropic or political, was rare [in 1911]. Co-education had been adopted by the provincial boards of education but a broad line of demarcation nevertheless existed between the activities of men and women. Public opinion accepted domestic duties as constituting the one correct sphere for women, but only a few of the more far-sighted ones were alive to their fight to receive training for this calling.

Canadian institutions refused to take advantage of Miss Ravenhill's knowledge and experience, forcing her to accept periodic appointments in the more liberal United States. As Miss Ravenhill's case shows, a woman in Canada still needed extraordinary courage, determination, and talent to break into the professional world.

There were, moreover, various sociological, cultural, and economic factors that not only kept the nineteenth-century woman in her place but that are still, if one looks closely, very much operative today.

Teaching was the first profession to open its doors to women. This breakthrough, however, was not the mark of a new progressiveness, but strictly the product of circumstance. As there was a shortage of male teachers, a few hard-pressed school boards began to hire women in the 1840's. Despite the need for teachers, custom and prejudice were not to be changed overnight and the boards' decision soon brought its own hardships and difficulties for the women who took advantage of it. Many parents, for instance, were doubtful whether a woman could keep order in the classroom, as a letter published in the sixties in the *Peterborough Examiner* pointed out. "There was great objection to the first lady teacher, Miss Lottie Heaslip, 1885 to 1887. Some of the parents even went so far as to have their children taken to another school because they did not see how a lady could keep discipline or be capable of teaching."

School boards, for their part, felt called upon to explain their apparent breach of tradition in hiring women and declared that it was no more than "a temporary measure" calculated "to tide them over a period of crisis." Women teachers, however incompetent, were better than no teachers. Also, for school trustees fighting to meet rising education costs, women teachers had the obvious advantage of saving the board money since they were paid much lower rates than men. In *The Development of Education in Canada*, Dr. C.E. Phillips calculated that "women received less than 60 per cent as much as men in 1860, about 75 per cent as much in 1900 and about 80 per cent as much in 1950."

Provincial governments, who did not share the economic advantages of the measure, echoed public disapproval of women teachers and instituted regulations to stem the flow of women into the public school system. They set a limit on the number of women teachers allowed in each parish and cut grants to schools that employed women. However, the struggle to staff the rapidly expanding school system only intensified with time, encouraging boards to hire women in increasing numbers and forcing provincial governments to withdraw their restrictions. By 1900, women teachers outnumbered men teachers five to one, completely reversing the situation of the early 1800's and creating another public outcry.

When the Normal School, legislated by the Ontario government in 1841 for "the training of young men...as teachers and instructors," finally opened its doors in 1847, its students inevitably included many women, setting the trend for the rest of the country. By 1860, women were a common sight in normal schools across the country, signalling the fact that women teachers – whatever their status in the community – were there to stay.

But circumstances such as the shortage of teachers did not always favour women. Since there was no shortage of male candidates in other professions, they admitted women into their precincts only after a prolonged and difficult struggle. Such was the case with the medical profession in the 1860's. Its members, as well as many of the general public, held that is was unladylike to discuss the "intimate," "mysterious," and "private" parts of the body in mixed company, and immodest for women even to *want* to study such a subject. Moreover, they felt that women were ill-suited and ill-equipped for the concentrated work required. Young ladies of good family were considered "frail tremulous creatures, given to weeping and swooning and fits of 'the Vapours,' ready to wilt before any difficult situation and totally incapable of facing the hardships of life." Medical school itself seemed threatening enough for sensitive creatures; the young women would have to dissect human bodies to learn anatomy and listen to lectures on many topics that might prove embarrassing. Besides, professors feared that the presence of women in class would prevent "a full and free discussion of some subjects." So pervasive were these views that it was not until 1883, some twenty years after her mother had fought unsuccessfully to get accepted into Medical School at the University of Toronto, that Augusta Stowe became the first woman to graduate in medicine in Canada.

There were, however, a few women who remained undeterred in face of all restrictions. Women such as Emily Howard Stowe and Maude Abbott were determined, intelligent, and self-confident enough to withstand the opposition and unpleasantness in their paths. Mrs. Stowe, born in 1831, had been brought up by parents who believed in the equality of sexes, and she was incensed by the University of Toronto Medical School's restrictions barring women, but fortunately, was among those women who could raise enough money to go to the United States to study. In 1865, leaving her three children with a sister, she enrolled in the New York Medical College of Women. Following her graduation in 1867, she returned to Toronto to practise, but found that her difficulties were far from over: the Council of the College of Physicians and Surgeons of Ontario refused to grant her a licence to practise. It was a vicious circle; the regulations stipulated that graduates from the United States had to attend one session of lectures at a recognized Ontario medical school and pass a set of examinations; yet no Ontario medical school would admit women students in 1867, not even for one session.

Dr. Stowe, nonetheless, was determined to practise, which

she did, becoming the first Canadian woman to practise medicine in this country. The fine for practising without a licence was $100, but there is no record whether or not Dr. Stowe was actually fined. Since she practised for thirteen years without a licence one can only assume that the College did not enforce its regulations too firmly.

In the meantime, Emily Stowe continued to apply regularly to various medical schools in Ontario, and for the next three years they continued to turn her down. Finally, in the early 1870's the University of Toronto Medical School agreed to allow Dr. Stowe and a Dr. Jennie Trout, who had also trained in the United States, to attend one session, provided they agreed to make no fuss if anti-feminist and embarrassed students or professors were rude. Emily agreed and stuck to her promise in spite of the fact that students and professors alike tried to embarrass and intimidate her whenever they could. However, after the humiliations she had endured and the prejudice she had encountered among fellow doctors, she flatly refused to comply with the second requirement – an oral examination before a panel of male doctors. She was convinced that the doctors – all of whom were reputed to be anti-feminists – would not be fair to a woman candidate. Her fears were to be echoed later by other women doctors like Dr. Elizabeth Matheson, who had graduated in 1898 from medical school, and refused to sit the examination to qualify her to practise in the Northwest Territories. In any event, because of Dr. Stowe's obstinacy, it was not until July 1880 that Emily Stowe was granted a licence to practise. In practical terms, her new official status had little bearing on her already successful career. By that time, she had established a large and lucrative practice, bought her family a home on Church Street in Toronto, and even put her husband through dentistry.

Dr. Stowe's success as a doctor, and that of other women doctors who began graduating from Canadian medical schools in 1883, appeared to have very little effect on anti-feminist attitudes in the medical profession or, for that matter, in other professions. Clara Brett Martin's application to the Law Society of Upper Canada in 1892 was just as strongly contested as Emily Stowe's application had been. For the most part, lawyers agreed "that the legal profession will not be benefited by the admission of ladies to its ranks." As one editor argued,

> There is some reason for the admission of women to the medical profession, but we know of no public advantage to admit them to the Bar, whilst there are many serious objections on grounds which are scarcely necessary to refer to. As a matter of taste it is rather a surprise to most men to see a woman seeking a profession where she is bound to meet much that would offend the natural modesty of her sex.

In spite of such overt prejudice, Clara Brett Martin, who was born in Toronto in 1874 and had graduated from Trinity College in 1890 taking high honours in Mathematics, immediately afterwards petitioned the Benchers to be entered as a "student of the laws." After appointing a special committee to consider her application, the Law Society turned her down five months later on the basis that it had no authority to admit women to membership. Miss Martin was politely informed that she must either abandon her ambition to practise law or move to the United States where women were admitted to the profession without any difficulty.

Clara Brett Martin settled for neither alternative. She appealed to the Attorney-General of Ontario, Sir Oliver Mowat, with the result that an Act was passed providing that the Law Society of Ontario could admit women to the study and practise of law, but only as solicitors not barristers. The Law Society, however, still refused to admit a woman. In desperation, Miss Martin appealed once again to the Attorney-General who, in turn, pressured the Law Society to admit women as solicitors. At last, Clara Brett Martin became a student of law. During her three years of articling with the well-known Toronto firm of Mulock, Miller, Crowther and Montgomery, she continued to fight for women's right to practise as barristers, with the result that she was admitted to the bar in February 1897, becoming the first woman barrister in Canada. Almost immediately she entered into partnership with the legal firm of Sheldon and Walbridge where she worked until her death in October 1923.

E. Cora Hind, who was eventually to become an editor on the *Winnipeg Free Press*, did not fare much better when, as a young women of twenty, she applied for the job of reporter on that paper in 1881. A newcomer to the city, Cora had a letter of introduction to the editor and naively expected to be given a job. The editor was shocked. "It would never do to have a woman in the newspaper business – a business that was marked by hard, rough work, late hours, and sometimes involved meeting not quite nice people." Disappointed but undeterred, Cora Hind applied her considerable energies in a different direction which, however, led her back to the newspaper and the job of agricultural editor on the *Free Press* twenty years later. Aggressive, ingenious, and intuitive, the young Cora foresaw the need for typists in the developing West, so she rented a typewriter, taught herself to type, and soon became the first female typist west of Port Arthur. After three years she branched out on her own and started a typists' bureau. During the next few years Cora was kept busy covering and writing up reports on agricultural meetings for her clients. In time, she began writing on various aspects of agriculture which won her a reputation in the agricultural community for her amazing ability to estimate the wheat crop.

This expertise had tremendous implications for, in the days before the Canadian Wheat Board took over marketing, wheat prices fluctuated widely according to the size and quality of the crop. Crop prediction was, therefore, of vital concern not only to the economy of the West but to that of Canada and the United States as well. It was Cora's reputation as a "fortune teller" that eventually won her the job she had always wanted. Woman or not, the new editor of the *Free Press* saw her as a valuable asset and she became agricultural editor of the paper in 1901.

Other women faced the same prejudices as Cora Hind, Clara Martin, and Emily Stowe when they tried to enter new fields. Even when they succeeded in breaking down the barriers barring them from professional training, they generally found that their troubles were far from over and that their careers were constantly obstructed.

Although teaching had become respectable for young women by the 1870's, it hardly offered an easy life to those who chose it. Both the general public and school boards were fond of flaunting their contempt for the profession and its members. The preponderance of women in the profession continued to be deplored on the grounds that women could not give the moral guidance nor reflect the kind of image children needed. As late as 1904, one school superintendent objected: "We used to have men and women in charge of our public schools. Now we have...mainly girls...Boys from twelve years of age upwards need a man's guidance and control to develop them properly." A year later, President Burwash of the University of Toronto urged "that ten years of age be set as the upper limit for a boy to be under a woman teacher." Newspapers, too, continued to express the public concern that "teaching, once a stern masculinity whose symbol was the blue beech gad, has become a Tennysonian feminine idyll whose motto is moral suasion."

The women who had struggled to become doctors and lawyers suffered even greater harassment, partly because their professions, unlike teaching, were not necessarily related to children. It is not surprising that after these women graduated many worked in fields related to women and children, thereby avoiding a degree of the aspersion cast on them. Women doctors often became pediatricians or gynecologists, women lawyers had many women clients, and women magistrates and judges worked in juvenile and family courts. During their training, however, women in medicine, law, and even teaching suffered many unpleasant incidents which undoubtedly affected the course of their career once they graduated. During her fight to win women the right to become barristers, Clara Brett Martin told a reporter on the *Buffalo Express*:

If I weren't determined to open the way to the bar for others of my sex I would have given up the effort long ago. You would not believe how many obstacles I have had to overcome, single-handed. I was articled to one of the largest law firms in Toronto, and when I put in my appearance I was looked upon as an interloper, if not a curiosity. The clerks avoided me and made it as unpleasant for me as they possibly could, and for a time it looked as if I were doomed to failure through a source with which I had not reckoned. Finally, however, I had the satisfaction of beating them all in the examinations.

In a story in the *Montreal Daily Witness,* November 27, 1897, Faith Fenton elaborated on some of the humiliations Miss Martin was forced to endure and stated that the most trying was the "unnecessary emphasis upon certain lecture points in the thousand ways that men can make a woman suffer who stands among them alone." Professors and students alike emphasized points involving sex in an effort to embarrass Miss Martin.

When Martha Hamm Lewis succeeded in her fight to be admitted to the New Brunswick training school for teachers in the 1850's, the council warned her that it took no responsibility for any ill results. It soon became clear that no one was going to allow this lone female to disrupt classes in any way. "She had to enter the classroom ten minutes before the other students and was required to wear a veil. She was asked to sit alone at the back of the room, retire five minutes before the lecture ended, and leave the premises without speaking to the male students." And when the University of Toronto allowed Emily Stowe and Jennie Trout to attend lectures for one session, the two ladies were the victims of countless embarrassing incidents which were annoying and tiring even if most of them were on the level of schoolboy pranks. As one friend said: "on more than one occasion [their seats] had to be cleared and cleaned before being occupied; [students painted] obnoxious sketches on the wall [that] had to be whitewashed four times during that session and [lecturers told] needless objectionable stories to the class to instigate its worst element to make noise and vulgar demonstrations."

Despite the obstacles and prejudice that marred the professional lives of these women, most of them were financially successful in their profession and a few even distinguished themselves in their particular field. Cora Hind, for example, was granted an LL.D from the University of Winnipeg in tribute to her outstanding career. At a ceremony to honour her, the editor of the *Free Press* acknowledged her achievement: "As a specialist and authority in your particular field, you have built a reputation which is world-wide; and you could go nowhere where agricultural pursuits are intelligently followed, that you could not find [Cora Hind] a known and familiar name." Dr. Maude Abbott (1869-1919), a brilliant Montreal doctor, won international acclaim in the medical profession for her contribution to the knowledge and understanding of congenital cardiac anomalies. After studying many congenitally defective hearts, Dr. Abbott discovered similarities that allowed her to classify the defects by groups or types. Her discovery contributed greatly to the whole field of heart surgery by simplifying diagnoses. Dr. Abbot's position as curator of the McGill Medical Museum proved an enormous help in her research as she had access to hundreds of different specimens.

When she was appointed in the early 1900's she faced the monumental task of classifying and cataloguing specimens that had been collected ever since the medical college opened. The collection had been useless as a teaching aid to date as the material had never been organized, but through Dr. Abbott's work the museum became one of the outstanding collections in the world. Throughout her career, Dr. Abbott was sought as the authority on congenital heart conditions, autopsy specimens were sent to her from all over North America and Europe, and young cardiologists came to study under her. Yet, ironically, her presence failed to have any significant influence on male attitudes in Canada. Although McGill at last paid tribute to Dr. Abbott by awarding her an honorary degree, it continued to bar women from its medical school.

It was not until the end of the First World War that the urgent need for medical personnel led the university to relax its restrictions and open its doors to women. Although Dr. Abbott had been appointed curator of the Medical Museum of McGill in the early 1900's and had been invited to join the staff of several other medical schools, only in 1925 did McGill appoint her Assistant Professor of Medical Research, a position she held until her retirement. Previously, Dr. Abbott had accepted a two-year appointment as Professor of Pathology and Bacteriology at the Women's Medical College of Pennsylvania, but only on the condition that she was on loan from McGill. Dr. Abbott herself was loath to leave McGill, her beloved Alma Mater, however long it had taken to recognize her abilities and despite the fact that after graduating in Arts from McGill she had been forced to attend medical school at Bishop's because McGill refused to accept women.

The majority of these early professional women had many characteristics in common. With the odd exception, they all came from hard-working, clean-living, middle-class backgrounds, and, although in some cases money might have been scarce, values such as responsibility, work, and education played a prominent role in their upbringing. Emily Stowe's desire to become a doctor is not so unusual in view of her Quaker heritage. Although her parents had adopted Methodism as their religion, they clung to the values of the Society of Friends which stressed woman's equality with man. This doctrine had its effect on all the women in the family, for Emily's two sisters became doctors as well, although they remained in the United States to practise. In another generation, Emily Stowe's only daughter, Augusta, grew up to be an ardent feminist who became the first woman to graduate from a Canadian medical school. Likewise, Judge Emily Murphy's interest in women's rights can be traced to a home where boys and girls were expected to share responsibilities in exchange for equal opportunities. And, while an orphan on her grandfather's farm, Cora Hind was not discouraged from taking a keen interest in such masculine pastimes as farm management.

It was probably this early exposure to unorthodox views that was at least partly the source of these women's independent thinking and fierce individualism. Inevitably, they were regarded as eccentrics or at least "characters" by their contemporaries, and not altogether without foundation. Emily Stowe, for example, changed her religion from Methodist to what she called "scientific socialist" and insisted on being cremated upon her death for sanitary reasons. "I have never done an act on earth to pollute it," she told her daughter Augusta, "and I do not wish to do so in dissolution." Although this may not seem unusual today, very few people were cremated in 1903. As Montreal had the only crematorium in Canada at the time, Dr. Stowe's remains were shipped to Buffalo, New York, which was closer to Toronto.

Cora Hind also attracted her share of attention, especially when she was travelling across the West on her crop inspection tours. She would don high laced riding boots, riding breeches, a long duck coat, and soft khaki shirt – a costume that she justified on the grounds that it was easier to manage while climbing through wire fences. Farmers had many stories about the stangely clad Miss Hind and her even stranger work. Cora Hind used to travel thousands of miles by railway, buckboard and later by motor car "seeing the crops." She would often cover a couple of hundred miles a day and climb fifty fences as she would estimate a crop only after she had marched into the field to examine it in various places.

Significantly, few of these women who broke into new fields had any initial intention to work for women's rights, but after their struggle to gain admittance to their chosen professions, they became more aware of the unequal legal status of women in Canada. Their personal fights with authority often resulted in a determination to make women in Canada more conscious of their potential; but more important, perhaps, was the role played by women like Helen MacGill, Nellie McClung, and Emily Murphy, for they realized that the most effective way was to make governments and official bodies change the discriminatory legislation against women.

Emily Murphy (1868-1933).

CHAPTER EIGHT

Persons or Not:
The Legal Status of Women

As women obtained more education, whether in schools, universities, or through their experiences in jobs, they became increasingly aware of their position in society. They began to see women's lack of access to a proper education as one of the chief reasons for their subordinate position. Moreover, they realized that men were not going to change things for them; women themselves would have to and could break down the barriers. Women like Adelaide Hoodless, Nellie McClung, Helen Mac-Gill, and Emily Murphy were determined to work for positive change by giving girls in the schools and women in urban communities and rural areas the necessary facts on health measures, economics, and legal rights to raise the standard of living in their own homes and at least to be able to protect the few rights they did have.

It proved a long struggle, fought on many fronts and in many areas. Not only were Canadians resistant to change of any kind, but they were antagonistic towards women who meddled in affairs outside the home.

In the latter part of the century, when Adelaide Hoodless

tried to stamp out the appalling ignorance of good health practices, which had led to her own son's death and which was contributing to the high rate of infant mortality in eastern Canada, she faced bitter opposition. She was derided in the press and from the platform as "one of those despised women who should be home caring for her family." But despite such cruel attacks, Mrs. Hoodless carried on with her campaign, driven by the desire to educate women "with a special attention to sanitation...a better understanding of the economic and hygienic value of foods and a more scientific care of children with a view of raising the general standard of the life of farm people." Having been born and brought up on a farm herself, Mrs. Hoodless knew just how badly such education was needed. She realized that if she had been taught such simple health measures as boiling fresh milk for a baby, her child would not have died from drinking contaminated milk.

However indisputable Mrs. Hoodless's case appears to us now, the women of her time viewed it differently. Although one baby in five died, and every family had its share of graves to remind it of its losses, people were reluctant to embrace new ideas and practices. Many women could not understand Mrs. Hoodless's feelings of guilt over her baby's death. After all, they argued "death was almost inevitable in large families and it was useless to get so upset about it."

Born in 1858, the youngest of twelve children, Adelaide Hoodless was used to standing up for herself and was well able to shrug off the many unkind remarks and unflattering insinuations cast her way during her crusade for change. She also had the support of her husband, a successful, well-respected citizen of Hamilton. Nonetheless, the indifference, if not outright antagonism, on the part of other women made Mrs. Hoodless realize that she could not handle the task of teaching hygiene alone. If she wanted to make an impact on public opinion and awaken people to the need for educating women as homemakers, she would have to work through women's groups. Such groups, as Helen MacGill used to say, "were valuable vehicles for the propagation of new ideas regarding woman's role in society." For the same reasons as Judge MacGill had become an inveterate "joiner" of women's organizations out West, Mrs. Hoodless became prominent in several organizations for women, many of which she helped to form. Perhaps the most significant in her notable list of accomplishments was the role she played in starting the whole movement of Women's Institutes in 1897.

Mrs. Hoodless had seen how much men had benefited from the Farmers' Institutes that taught them the latest techniques in agriculture and gave them a place to discuss their problems, and she had the foresight to see that a similar type of organization could have similar benefits for rural women by providing them with knowledge and skills in homemaking. It was a new idea, especially in isolated rural areas where women did things about the house as their mothers and grandmothers had done before them and paid little attention to even the most basic health practices. Their windows remained tightly shut, food was cooked until no vitamins remained, and milk pails sat uncovered, inviting flies, dust, and dirt. And yet, before Mrs. Hoodless's efforts, no attempt had been made to teach girls and women proper health practices.

The first Women's Institute was established at Stoney Creek in 1897 and attracted some seventy-five members. Moreover, through Mrs. Hoodless's relentless lobbying, the Ontario government pledged to give the Women's Institutes the same money grants as it gave the Farmers' Institutes and offered to supply lecturers for their meetings.

After starting the Women's Institutes, she had worked to make domestic science classes an integral part of the curriculum in all public schools. When the success of these created a demand for teachers, she lobbied for the government to establish a training school to prepare teachers in domestic science.

Then in 1910, while she was giving a speech at Massey Hall in Toronto to raise money and support for a course in domestic science at a Canadian university, Adelaide Hoodless dropped dead. Her last speech was not in vain, however, for a year after her death the Lillian Massey School of Household Science opened in Toronto and, while not named after Mrs. Hoodless, it marked the fulfilment of her dream.

Adelaide Hoodless's life-long crusade to make women better homemakers did not clash with other crusades for women's rights in the professions. Most of these women, like Helen Mac-Gill, Nellie McClung, and Emily Murphy, saw woman's role in society as an extension of her fundamental role as wife and mother. Whereas Mrs. Hoodless had worked to equip women to be better homemakers, other women of her day tried to teach them about the need for women's suffrage. Just as it had taken the death of her son to awaken Adelaide Hoodless to the need to educate other women, many suffragettes had to be jolted into an awareness of the problem as Nellie McClung was during her first years teaching on the Prairies and Emily Murphy was after she moved west in 1903.

Emily Murphy

For three months in the summer of 1929, Canada's more liberal-minded women waited uneasily for news from England
that would dramatically influence the status of Canadian
women in the future. In England, five judges of the Judicial
Committee of the Privy Council, headed by the Lord Chancel-
lor, pondered hundreds of articles of constitutional law in an
effort to determine whether or not women could legally be considered "persons" under the provisions of the British North
America Act. Between 1917 and 1928, five successive Canadian
governments had considered that women were not "persons"
under the meaning of the B.N.A. Act and therefore were ineligible
for a seat in the Senate. The arguments of these governments
were based on the point that the various provisions of the B.N.A.
Act had to be given the same construction as that which the
courts would have given when the Act was first passed in 1867.
Despite government promises to look into the matter, years had
passed with no change. At last, in 1929 the matter was before
the Privy Council thanks to the efforts of a group of determined
Canadian women led by one of Canada's great crusaders for
social justice, Emily Ferguson Murphy.

Emily Murphy might never have turned her attention to
this issue had it not been for an incident that occurred on her
first day in court in September 1916. As the first woman in the
British Empire to be appointed to the position of Police Magistrate, Emily Murphy had roused the anger of anti-feminists. In
an article for *Maclean's* in 1920, some three years later, she
wrote that she had just finished handing down a rather stiff
sentence to a bootlegger when his defence counsel, Eardley
Jackson, turned on her: "You're not even a person!" he
shouted. "You have no right to be holding court!" Taken
aback, the surprised magistrate asked the counsel to elaborate:
"Under British common law," he explained, "in a decision

handed down in 1876, the status of women is this:'Women are persons in matters of pains and penalties, but are not persons in matters of rights and privilege.' Since the office of Magistrate is a privilege, the present incumbent is here illegally. No decisions of her court can be binding." And on those words, he strode out of court.

Although she had found her first day in court "as pleasant an experience as running a rapids," Emily discovered that it had been mild in comparison to the days ahead. "On every subsequent case," she recalled, "this man [Eardley Jackson] who is the most popular criminal lawyer in the city, persisted in raising the objection, while I persisted in hearing the whole argument."

These incidents continued for four years, until in 1920 the Honourable Mr. Justice Scott of the Supreme Court of Alberta settled the matter as far as that province was concerned by ruling that, in his opinion, women were "persons."

Frustrated and inconvenienced as she was by the issue, Emily waited in the hope that the federal government would act voluntarily on the matter, as promised, and rule that women were indeed "persons" under the B.N.A. Act. For seven years she watched as successive governments in Ottawa ignored, hedged, and evaded the issue. Various national women's groups had requested that a woman be appointed to the Senate. This, in effect, would have settled the matter since Section 24 of the B.N.A. Act stated that "the Governor-General shall from time to time in the Queen's name...summon qualified persons to the Senate; and subject to the provisions of this act, every person so summoned shall become and be a member of the Senate, and a Senator." In 1917 the women's groups went a step further and recommended Emily Murphy for the appointment. She agreed to let her name go forward for the Senate, and from that time on, Emily began to work on the case, seeking legal advice on how to fight the federal government's interpretation of the word "persons" in the B.N.A. Act. Finally, it was one of her brothers, a judge in Ontario, who informed her that the

B.N.A. Act's ambiguous and inconsistent use of the third person that obviously referred to women in some instances allowed for a different interpretation – one that included women in the category of "persons." Emily also learned that Section 60 of the Supreme Court Act permitted any five or more interested persons, appealing as a unit, to ask for the interpretation of a constitutional point raised under the British North America Act. If the Department of Justice agreed that the question was of sufficient public importance, it would be referred by the Governor-General-in-Council to the Supreme Court and would pay all "reasonable fees" arising from the case on behalf of the appellants. After many letters asking confirmation of her brother's interpretation of this section of the Act, Mrs. Murphy settled on the five Alberta women she would ask to sign the petition. She chose Nellie McClung, a close friend and noted author, public speaker, and women's rights worker; Irene Parlby, the only woman member of the Alberta Cabinet; Louise McKinney, a former member of the Provincial Legislature, and Henrietta Muir Edwards, convenor of Laws for the National Council of Women.

The "persons" case opened in Ottawa on March 14, 1928, and, despite predictions that it would be over within the hour, it lasted all day. The Honourable N.W. Rowell, K.C., argued the case for the five appellants, and the Attorney-General of Canada, representing the Crown, argued against the petition, as the government had taken the stand that women could not be considered persons within the meaning of the B.N.A. Act and that an amendment would be necessary before a woman could be summoned to the Senate. Since all the provinces were treaty partners in the B.N.A. Act and, as such, concerned with the official interpretation of any section of it, they were offered the opportunity of sending a representative to put forward their position on the question. Only two provinces, Alberta and Quebec, were interested enough to take up the offer. Alberta supported the appellants, and Quebec argued against them, which was not surprising as the women of Quebec did not get the provincial vote until 1940.

Judgement was reserved for five weeks at the end of which a telegram from Mr. Rowell on April 24, 1928, brought Emily the disappointing news: "Regret Supreme Court have answered question submitted to them in the negative." The judgement read by Chief Justice Anglin, based its conclusions on the principle that the meaning of the B.N.A. Act must be interpreted in the light of conditions existing in 1867. Two important facts had a direct bearing on the judgement. The office of Senator was first created by the B.N.A. Act; and women were legally incapable of holding public office at the time the Act was passed. Therefore, the word "persons" as used in Section 24 of the B.N.A. Act did not include women. The Chief Justice went on to point out that in 1868, a year after the British North America Act became law, one of England's learned judges had "excused [women] from taking any share in public affairs."

"There can be no doubt about it," Mr. Justice Anglin concluded, "that the word 'persons' when standing alone, includes women. It connotes human beings – the criminal and the insane, equally with the good and wise citizen; the minor as well as the adult. Hence the propriety of the restrictions placed on its use in this section (24) which speaks of 'fit and qualified' persons. The terms in which the qualifications of members of the Senate are specified...import that only men are eligible for appointment." However, the day the negative decision was announced, the government also announced that "it would immediately set steps in motion for the amendment of the B.N.A. Act to include women in the Senate."

Emily was not impressed; she realized all too well how difficult this would be in view of the fact that any change in the B.N.A. Act required the agreement of all the provinces. When Parliament made no sign of fulfilling its promise, Emily decided to appeal the question in the Privy Council, and in July 1929, the question "Are women Persons?" came before the august body of judges who formed the highest court in the British Empire. Much as she would have liked to listen to the case in London, Emily decided it was wiser to stay in Canada. In a letter to the four other appellants she explained that the inevitable social contacts with women's groups in England might harm their cause.

> In [my] mind we would be identifying ourselves with a group which, while non-partisan in character, is yet making strenuous efforts for the admission of peeresses in their own right to the House of Lords. While heart and soul in sympathy with their fight, I feel it would not be good policy to confuse the legal, political or public minds of Great Britain concerning our particular contention. While our ultimate aims are similar, our cases do not rest upon the same bases and we would not be well advised in drawing upon our case any hostility that might have arisen against theirs.

Judgement was reserved following the July hearing of the case and summer faded into autumn without a decision. Finally, on October 18, Emily's phone rang at 3:00 a.m. Lifting the receiver she heard the news she had been waiting to hear for thirteen years. The Privy Council had decided that the law should apply to circumstances as they arise; women were to be considered as "persons." With jubilant cries of "We've won, we've won!" Emily wakened the rest of the household. The next day telegrams of congratulation poured into the Murphy house from across the country. Nellie McClung's comment, "The victory belongs to Mrs. Murphy whose handling of the whole matter has been a masterpiece of diplomacy," summarized the general feeling.

People who knew Emily Murphy were not surprised that she had won her case. As one reporter for the *Edmonton Journal* described her in 1910, "This leader of women will keep hammering away until even the most obstinate man will be convinced that it is best to withdraw and quietly let down the bars." He was not exaggerating. Emily's rigorous efforts to initiate improvements in public life had won her a reputation as a fighter. "Whenever I don't know whether to fight or not – I always fight," became one of her favourite slogans and apparently a successful one, since many of her fights brought long-sought and much-needed reform legislation, among which the Dower Act of 1911 figured prominently. This Act provided that a wife must get a third of her husband's estate even if he did not leave a will and that it was impossible for him to will away her third of the property. It was a great win for women in Alberta who had previously had no legal claim to any of their husband's money. "Time and time again I have heard the bitter story of a woman who had worked with her man for years on a piece of land, only to have him sell out suddenly and go off with some other woman," she recalled.

With this same determination, Emily had fought for improved hospital conditions, although this crusade had started more or less by chance. Emily was asked to be "the name" on a ladies' committee which made an annual inspection of the local hospital. On the day of the inspection, she refused to remain in the cordoned-off area that the ladies were shown and instead popped into the kitchen to question the cook, wandered through wards to talk with patients, and peered behind closed doors and even into cupboards for tell-tale signs of inefficiency. Her efforts were well rewarded. When she handed in her report, which was published in the *Edmonton Bulletin* in 1910, "she launched an uproar that was to rock Edmonton for years" and which would result in much needed changes. Among other things she noted that access to fire escapes was blocked by beds, the nurses' diningroom was next to the mortuary ("Comment unnecessary," remarked Mrs. Murphy), and the hospital was running on a daily deficit of nearly a hundred dollars.

Emily's background prepared her well for her role as leader of social reform. As a writer and the wife of a parson, she had gained considerable experience in observing and dealing with people. In "My Career as a Parson's Wife," an unpublished record of these years, Emily told how "as a bride of nineteen, [she] had to take Bible classes, be president of the missionary society, play the organ, speak at meetings, [and] organize the entertainments and bazaars." These activities varied little in the different parishes where the young couple lived and, after her four daughters were born, Emily was quite content to enjoy her role as wife and mother in the financial security, social stability, and pastoral serenity typical of small-town life in Western Ontario at the end of the last century.

But Arthur became restless and anxious to put his considerable gift for preaching to greater use. When he asked his wife to exchange the stability and security she had always known for the economic uncertainty and rootlessness of missionary life, Emily agreed, little suspecting the long-term effects of her decision.

For the next two years, Arthur and Emily lived in hotels and stayed with local ministers' families while Arthur toured his new diocese in Huron County, Ontario. Although their three girls and a nurse travelled with them much of the time, Emily had none of her former household responsibilities or church work to occupy her. Apart from some necessary social appearances at teas and suppers, she found that she had disconcertingly long periods of free time. Although she met hundreds of people, she had little opportunity to develop friends and confidants. It seemed natural that she should turn to writing as a hobby and an outlet.

At first she wrote sketches of the people she met and, in the evenings, would read them to her husband to divert him after a long day's work. His reactions were so favourable that Emily soon found herself consciously striving to write more clearly and amusingly. Eager for new material, she took a new interest in the people around her, enquiring into their lifestyles and their motives for doing things, and learning how to put people at their ease so that they would confide in her.

By the time Arthur was invited to take his family to England to preach for the winter of 1898, Emily's skill as a writer had improved considerably. On her return to Toronto she published her impressions of the year abroad. *Janey Canuck Abroad,* poorly printed, badly proof-read, and generally an unimpressive-looking book, still got favourable reviews in England and

the United States because of its fresh, frank, nationalistic out-
look. This tone, in fact, was no more than a reflection in print of
Emily Murphy's strong identity as a Canadian. During her
year abroad, she had happened to overhear some Englishmen
complaining that "Canadians had the same nasal monotone
and tiresome habit of bragging as the Americans." Leaning
forward Emily said: "Maybe. But do you recall that one of
your own countrywomen – Miss Isabelle Baird (sic) who has
travelled the world for many years – gave the interesting decision that while Americans are naturally assumptive, the English are personally so!"

Emily's lifelong ability to see through the veneer of tradition, pomp, and ceremony also became evident at this time.
After hearing the Archbishop of Canterbury preach a particularly boring sermon, she commented, "I have a shrewd suspi-
cion that a Canadian parish in the back countries would probably starve him out." And instead of being impressed, as a good
colonial should be, by such traditionally English pastimes as
grouse-shooting, she described the sport as "savouring much of
the potting of chickens in a farm-yard, since the game was so
plentiful."

On the other hand, Emily found much to interest her in
England, particularly the cosmopolitan crowds that contrasted
so vividly with the familiar homogeneous population of small
Ontario towns. Here, for the first time in her life, Emily was
exposed to a world full of poverty, degradation, and relentless
exploitation; and here, for the first time, she showed her desire
to help. When accompanying Arthur on his visits to slum areas
in London, Emily provoked the local curate by her compas-
sionate remarks. "Really, Mrs. Murphy," he chided her. "It
does not do to get too familiar with these people." Frustrated
by the curate's belief in prayer as the only solution to such
problems as poverty and disease, Emily later wrote, "Whose
responsibility was it, if not the ministers'? There is not much
use in preaching to people whose spirits are deadened by hardships and starvation, and who are struggling to keep their foot-
ing in a quicksand."

After their trip abroad, the Murphys returned to Toronto. The next few years were not easy ones for the family. The first blow came when Arthur collapsed backstage after making a speech at Massey Hall. Sitting in the front row, Emily had sensed something was wrong. He had a reputation for being an articulate and forceful speaker, yet now she saw he was groping for words as if his mind were on other things. As she pushed her way backstage the audience's criticism added to her suspicions: "What's there about him that's so good? He might have been all right for the counties but you expect something more in Toronto..." Arthur's collapse was due to typhoid. Emily helped to nurse him for weeks, but with a full-time nurse and the ordinary household expenses, she was constantly plagued by financial worries. Then, while he was still sick, the Church Parochial Mission informed her that "financial difficulties forced them to curtail their Mission work...[and] they would have to terminate their arrangement with the Rev. Arthur Murphy." Now in serious financial difficulties, Emily wrote article after article for the *National Monthly*, a new Toronto magazine for which she had been writing since her return from England, and of which she was soon appointed women's editor. Fortunately, the magazine was eager for all she could give them, and Emily's only trouble was finding time to write. Her husband had no sooner recovered than she came down with the disease herself and had to spend weeks in hospital. However, with typical resilience, as soon as she was well enough to be propped up on pillows, Emily wrote "The Diary of a Typhoid Patient," which she promptly sold to help pay her expenses.

But the Murphy's troubles were not over yet. In November 1902, while she and Arthur were still weak from typhoid, their youngest daughter, Doris, aged nine, became suddenly ill with diphtheria. With her husband away at the time, Emily had to nurse the child alone. When Doris died, Emily scribbled out the stark news to wire to her husband: "Doris just died. Come. Membraneous croup." Doris was the second child the Murphys had lost, for another daughter had died as a nine-month-old baby a few years earlier. This second death came at a bad time for Arthur, who, already weakened by typhoid, remained so despondent and physically debilitated that his doctor recommended an outdoor life as his only hope for full recovery. The Murphys decided to move west to Swan River, a small town some two days' train ride from Winnipeg, where Arthur planned to cut and sell lumber. Emily, too, felt the need to get away, and hoped that a new setting would provide fresh stimulus for her writing which had developed considerably in the past years. Already an author of some note after the success of *Janey Canuck Abroad* and her numerous articles for the *National Monthly*, she was looking for new material which she thought she would find in the West.

She could not have chosen a more fortuitous, or more profitable, time to write about the West. As over a million new settlers poured into the Prairies between 1901 and 1911, they created an expanding market for all commodities, including books, and in particular books about the opening up of the West.

Swan River turned out to be a drab, sprawling town strung out along the railway. It was like many other embryonic western settlements of that era which had sprung up in the wake of the railway. At first glance it had little to commend it. Emily hated the "hideous, box-like houses" covered inside and out with tin and the flimsy false fronts on the few stores. But despite the shabbiness of the town and its isolation, Emily succumbed to the spirit of the place and soon surprised her friends in the East with her enthusiastic reports: "There is a magic in this land, and you can hear unsung things. My heart is on tip-toe for reach of them." She grew almost to pity those still in the East: "How unfortunate are the ones who live in the Eastern provinces. Existence there is only canned life. We of the West belong to the select few."

With her husband away much of the time and her two daughters in boarding school in Winnipeg, Emily had time to roam the countryside and the surrounding towns, talking to the people and learning about their different customs and their problems in adjusting to a new land and, in some cases, a new culture. At night she filled her notebooks with the accounts and experiences of the day. These sketches of frontier life were to become famous for, after the Murphys left Swan River in 1907, Emily changed a few names and published them in 1910 as *Janey Canuck in the West.* The book was hailed by critics and public alike as one of the most successful and delightful accounts of life in the developing West.

When Arthur decided he wanted to have a look at what lay further West in the new province of Alberta (which had only joined the Dominion of Canada in 1904), Emily agreed, but somewhat reluctantly: "The Padre had decided to live in Edmonton, and I have decided to remain in Swan River. We will compromise on Edmonton," she joked.

Whatever her feelings had been originally, Emily soon came to love Edmonton. Residents welcomed and entertained her as an author of note and she found herself enjoying the social life of the city. "It's a great place, this Canadian West," she wrote. "It's a country of strong men, straight living, and hard riding...We're very socially inclined with teas, tennis, mobiling, dancing, dining and wild riding across the hills. When people are healthy and prosperous, they are instinctively hospitable and always in a big-handed, big-hearted way."

It wasn't long before Emily developed great plans for the city's future. She caused endless confusion among her visitors by giving her address as 11011 - 88th Avenue. On one occasion, she opened the door to find an astonished English journalist who had expected number 11011 to be on a street lined with houses. "If this is 11011, where are the other hundreds?" she inquired. "Oh, them? Going to be built!" cried Emily, and proceeded to deliver her usual speech about the city's future. As usual, Emily's idealism had led her to exaggerate, but there was more than a vestige of truth in what she said. In the first seven years of the century, Edmonton's population had increased from 4,000 to 14,000, creating a feeling of excitement among its residents. Soon after she arrived in Edmonton, Emily wrote "It is good to live in these first days when the foundations of things are being laid, to be able, now and then, to place a stone or carry the mortar to set it good and true." Setting it "good and true" meant to her eradicating the many social ills spawned by rapid urbanization.

The next few years were agreeably but uneventfully occupied with social work and writing. Then, in 1916, a courtroom incident disrupted Emily's routine life. Two delegates from the Law Committee of the Local Council of Women were asked to leave a courtroom where some women were to be tried in a case of prostitution. Reluctant as they were to leave, they were shamed into it when counsel for the Crown remarked that "decent women such as they appeared to be, could have no desire to hear evidence in these cases." The women called Mrs. Murphy for advice. "Agree with the magistrate," she told them. "Such cases should not be heard by a mixed audience. And apply immediately to the government, urging that a court be established for the City of Edmonton in which women offenders may be tried by a woman in the presence of women." As had happened so often in similar instances, the women asked Emily to take their case to the government. Emily agreed and took the case to the Attorney-General. To her surprise, the Attorney-General not only agreed that such a court was urgently needed but asked her whether she was ready to be sworn in. Totally taken aback, Emily tried to disqualify herself. "I'm not ready at all," she replied. "I've never thought of this. I don't know anything...What about my writing?" She finally agreed to go home and think about it and consult her husband who encouraged her to accept: "It's an office you can assume with dignity and in which you can serve your country-women more closely." She also consulted a few of her close friends and her two daughters, all of whom urged her to accept. The fact that she had had no legal training was unimportant as laymen were frequently appointed to the bench at that time. One aspect of the job, however, bothered Emily. "I was afraid of the nastiness of sex-pedlary that would have to be considered even before a court made up largely of women." In her Victorian upbringing, she explained, "it was not considered good form to mention an animal of the opposite sex by name, therefore, equines and bovines were all one sex to me. While I could write of matters relating to sexual problems, I found it difficult to speak of them even to my own children." However, Emily eventually pushed this personal qualm aside and accepted the job. She was sworn in on July 1, 1916 becoming the first woman in the British Empire to be appointed Police Magistrate.

To a conscientious and humane woman, the role of judge was often difficult. To begin with, Judge Murphy read widely on the subject and often spent hours at a time in the court library pouring over legal volumes. As she struggled to gain a firm grasp of the law, she became aware that her activities were increasingly hampered by petty restrictions and difficulties. She could not get proper furniture for her office; she was not given sufficient staff; she could not get a key to her desk or a police badge without time-consuming hassles. When she realized that this was the work of a small body of anti-feminist men who resented her intrusion into what had previously been all-male territory, Emily decided to keep the matter to herself. She did not want to risk being labelled as a difficult and emotionally unstable woman trying to encroach on male-dominated fields.

While Judge Murphy fought these petty battles backstage, she tried to acquaint herself with the strange new world of prostitutes, drug addicts, pregnant schoolgirls, mentally deficient adults, and mistreated children. Page after page of Emily's reports tell the stark facts she discovered behind the facade of conventional city life. But she was perhaps most appalled by the drug addicts she saw daily.

> Six years ago, when appointed a Police Magistrate and Judge of the Juvenile Court at Edmonton...I was astonished to learn that there was an illicit traffic in narcotic drugs of which I had been almost unaware and of which the public were unaware.

In an effort to learn more about all aspects of the drug trade,

Emily made several visits to areas where people indulged freely in opium and other narcotics.

> Several years ago, with two plain clothes men...I visited Chinatown in Vancouver...In entering Shanghai Alley, I was warned to stand clear of the doorways lest a rush be made from inside, when I would be trampled upon. In passing up a narrow staircase of unplaned boards one detective walked ahead and one behind me, each carrying a flashlight. "Why do you keep me between you?" I asked...Without replying, the head man stopped about midway up, and inserted a long key into a board when, to my amazement, a door opened where no door had been visible. Here, in a small cupboard, without a window — a kennel of a place — lay four opium debauchees, or, as the police designate them, "hop-heads." The hole was absolutely dark and the men slept heavily...plainly narcotized...And so, in like manner several doors were opened for me...As you looked and looked again on these prostrate, open-eyed insensates it began to dawn on you what Bret Harte meant when he spoke of "The dread valley of the shadow of the drug."

As she grew more familiar with drug addiction and trafficking, Emily became convinced that this social problem could only be stemmed with the help of an informed public. She wrote in *The Black Candle* (1922), her study of the drug trade in Canada, people must know "that there are men and women who batten and fatten on the agony of the unfortunate drug addict - palmerworms and human caterpillars who should be trodden underfoot like the despicable grubs that they are."

Emily's insight into the meaning of disease, viciousness, insanity, and cruelty grew daily. "In the courthouse one learns sad things," she wrote, "terrible things that may not be written down on paper, and that many would not dare to read. One feels that nothing can ever thrive again which is good or pure."

As a writer Emily could always retreat to write about rather than deal first-hand with the problems she encountered. As a judge, however, Emily found herself torn between a desire to do what was best for the people brought before her and the responsibilities of her position. There was, also, always the possibility of making an erroneous judgement. The first woman she sentenced to jail went insane and committed suicide after she was transferred to a mental asylum. Emily wrote that "the magistrate does not sleep so easefully if she has misgivings concerning the [mentally deranged people] whom she sent to prison, when these should properly be placed under custodial care of another kind."

The job presented other difficulties as well. Emily soon found that many women expected her to take their side at the expense of justice, and were surprised and resentful when she "sided with" a man. From time to time, Emily had cases of severe husband-beating. "He's able to take care of himself," was the usual excuse given in court but all too often Judge Murphy found evidence to the contrary. One man had both his thumbs broken by his wife, and another received a deep gash above the eye. In such cases Emily usually discovered that the victims were innocent and, despite accusations of disloyalty to her sex, she sentenced the offenders.

Nonetheless, Emily Murphy's activities in behalf of women's rights were considerable. Despite her belief that a woman's first responsibility was to produce healthy children, she was a firm advocate of a woman's right to seek fulfilment outside the domestic sphere. Moreover, she believed women had a specific role in the field of human justice. "If women can do nothing else in their new sphere," she wrote, "they can render service by interpreting the Senate to the public. Hitherto, it has only been reported...Women in the Senate could also serve the public by their work on the Divorce Committee...Women should at least be judged by one of their own sex who ought to possess an intimate understanding of domestic and marital difficulties."

In her heart, as her close friends knew, Emily longed to play that role. At sixty-two she had always won what she set out to attain and now had a serene confidence that she would, in time, be made the first woman Senator in Canada. Despite her considerable public achievements, her obviously happy marriage and family life, Emily Murphy died without achieving the one distinction she cherished – a seat in the Senate. After her role in the "person's" case, many people including Emily herself, half-expected that she would be made the first woman senator. Although she said nothing publicly, she hinted at her expectations in a letter to a friend: "Here's my new 'Who's Who'. It only needs the office of Senator!" Emily, however, was not to achieve this distinction. Towards the end of 1930 Prime Minister Mackenzie King did appoint a woman to the Senate, but he chose a well-known Liberal, Cairine Wilson. This partisan appointment shocked the women of the West, including Emily, who, in a letter to Howard Ferguson, Prime Minister for Ontario and an old family friend, confessed that she "made no unfavourable comment, but still found [herself] too ruffled in spirit to forward any congratulations to Ottawa." Publicly, however, Emily urged women "to rejoice that at last a woman sat in the Senate of Canada."

Later, when a vacancy for the Senate fell open in Edmonton, women once again wrote to Ottawa – this time to the Conservative Prime Minister, R.B. Bennett, – urging Emily's appointment and arguing that "no woman in Canada has given so freely of herself in the public service of her country and no woman is more worthy." But once again Emily Murphy was passed over with the argument that "recognition [had to be] given to a Roman Catholic." Only after Emily's death did the probable reason for her rejection come to light. Lotta Dempsey, women's editor of the *Edmonton Bulletin* at the time, asked one of the senators from Edmonton why they had never appointed Emily Murphy. "Murphy in the Senate!" he replied. "She would have caused too much trouble."

Emily's disappointment shows in the abruptness with which she ceased all reference to the Senate in her private papers, notes, and letters. In any case, at sixty-three and suffering from diabetes, she was beginning to slacken her pace at last. In 1930, Emily Murphy resigned as magistrate, retaining only her responsibilities in the Juvenile Court, and happily turned her attention to finishing her literary work. During her last two years, she spent the mornings in bed writing steadily at a large bed-table. She completed a paper on birth control entitled "Pruning the Family Tree," several articles on her work in prisons and asylums, and on public apathy towards venereal disease and prostitutes. Many of her afternoons were spent at the library researching the articles she never had time to write. On her last afternoon she was at the library, working on an attack on the c.c.f. That night, when her daughter Evelyn teased her about going to bed with her face all creamed up, she laughed and said, "Well, indeed, I'm not going to let myself get old and wrinkled!" She died peacefully in her sleep two hours later.

Thousands of people from all walks of life and backgrounds filed by her coffin, among them two prostitutes who placed a single rose on her hands. Evelyn Murphy left it there – a symbol of her mother's life-long crusade to help women, whoever they might be.

Claire Martin (1914-   ).

Thérèse Casgrain (1896-   ). PHOTO-CANADA WIDE

CHAPTER NINE

Women in Quebec

While, in the autumn of 1929, Emily Murphy and her supporters were celebrating the Privy Council's ruling that women
were officially "persons," a small body of women in the province of Quebec were still fighting for the right to vote in provincial elections – a right that had been granted to women in all
the other provinces of Canada by 1922. Mainly because women
lacked a political voice in Quebec, social legislation dealing
with women and children in that province lagged far behind
that of other provinces. For instance, whereas women in other
provinces had fought for and won basic property rights as early
as 1911, in 1940 married women in Quebec still remained economically dependent on their husbands, legally deprived of the
right not only to inherit property and own property they had
acquired, but even to lay claim to their own wages – all because
the Quebec Civil Code defined women as minors under the
authority of their husbands. Again, whereas women in other
parts of the country were readily admitted to the practice of
law – a move initiated in Ontario in 1897 – in 1940 women in
Quebec were still not admitted to the bar. And, while in the
rest of Canada adultery by either spouse was considered

grounds for divorce, in Quebec a man could divorce his wife for adultery but she could not divorce him on the same grounds unless he kept his lover under the same roof. As might be expected, these and many other disparities in the laws in Quebec prompted considerable comment from feminists across the country. They saw Quebec's backwardness in areas relating to women as proof that if women could not participate in public affairs there would be little social legislation. Moreover, they blamed Quebec women for not joining forces to fight for their rights.

For the most part, these critics failed to mention or appreciate the deep-rooted causes of Quebec women's inferior position in society. The English conquest of 1763 and the Church had both had a great influence on the French-Canadian people. Until the conquest, French Canadians had formed a small colony fighting for survival against nature and the hostile natives. But after their defeat on the Plains of Abraham in 1759, and the surrender of Montreal the following year, French Canadians found their difficulties compounded by their fear and antagonism towards the English who threatened to stamp out their culture, and by the psychological effects of having been betrayed by their mother country.

In *Convergences,* Jean Le Moyne notes that in the attempt to rationalize their situation, to help them survive in a foreign land, and to adjust to their role as deserted subjects, many of the French intelligentsia who remained in New France saw themselves as a "chosen race" with the mission to perpetuate true Catholicism, for they believed the faith had become perverted in Europe. With this mission, the Church and the state strove to keep their race from being absorbed by non-Catholic – that is to say, English – influences; and the philosophy commonly known as *la survivance* emerged as the dominating force in French Canada. Acting through the priests whose influence pervaded all aspects of their parishioners' lives, the Church encouraged and, when necessary, took steps to ensure that people stayed on the land away from the temptations and disruptive influences of the cities which eroded traditional values and dissipated the authority of the priests. The Church also emphasized that it was every French Canadian's duty to have as many children as possible to try to balance the population ratio of French to English.

Both men and women were affected by this Church-dominated life. Most grew up afraid to act against the dictates of the Church and the few who did were plagued by guilt. In *Les Insolences du Frère Untel,* published in 1960, Brother Jérôme points out that French Canadian men were psychologically emasculated in a world where they were not only members of a conquered race but pawns of an all-powerful clergy. The effects of this conditioning were so strong that they have persisted although many of the oppressive factors in the French Canadian's daily life have now disappeared. "We are afraid of authority," he wrote. "We live in a climate of magic under penalty of death, we must infringe no taboo, we must respect all the formulae, all the conformisms." Although French Canadian men were unquestionably masters in their own homes, they could expect little time from wives who had ten, twelve, or fourteen children to care for. Many sought release from their helpless rage and frustration with this system by lashing out against their underlings, whether they were wives, children, or employees. Often the women had little recourse in such instances for, under Quebec civil law, they had no rights. In fact, women in Quebec were treated more or less as work horses and broodmares; to their husbands they owed complete obedience; to the Church the "duty" to have as many children as possible. Reared on the doctrine that hell and damnation were the punishment for disobedience and defiance, Quebec women grew up psychologically ill-prepared to defy authority of any kind.

Even women writers like Marie Claire Blais, Anne Hébert, and Claire Martin were concerned with the needless suffering, poverty, and wasted lives that were the result of the Church's policies in Quebec. Of these writers, perhaps Claire Martin has painted the most vivid picture of the hard, warping childhood of many French Canadian girls.

Claire Martin

Born in Quebec City in 1914, Claire Martin was one of seven children of a prosperous engineer and his timid, insecure wife many years his junior. Theirs was "a marriage of a lion and a dove," as Claire put it. Only when she grew older did she learn that her mother had consented to such an unlikely match because at twenty-three she was still single and her parents were beginning to worry that she would never marry. She had had proposals from men in Montreal but she could not bring herself to leave her parents in Quebec. Claire saw many women of her mother's generation whose timidity, apprehension, inability to face life, and fear of the world and the hereafter resulted from the stifling and restrictive atmosphere of their day.

By the time Claire was four she was already aware of the "monstrousness" of her life among grownups who never spoke and children who did not dare ask questions. As Claire put it, "We were terrified to provoke our superiors who ruled with an iron glove slipped on over...an iron hand." As head of his family, her tyrannical father demanded submissiveness, servitude, and subjection from them all. "I am the master here," he told his children. "As if there could be any doubt" Claire used to think. A prosperous civil engineer, he was an archetypal figure of patriachal authority in Quebec. His very size gave him an advantage, for at six feet tall and 230 pounds he had little difficulty in forcing his will on his wife and children whom he beat regularly on the slightest provocation. Once, for instance, Claire stepped on his dog's paw by mistake and, "to teach her a lesson," her father stamped on her foot so hard she lost a nail and had a twisted toe for the rest of her life.

Another time, in an effort to help her exhausted mother, Claire tried to change the crying baby, but, being no more than a child herself, was unable to do up the diaper again and had left the baby naked in her crib. Her father had followed her into the baby's room and, finding the child naked, gave Claire a thorough beating. In a house where no one dared mention "buttocks" or "sexual parts," it was unthinkable that they should be left exposed, and Claire had to be made to realize that she had committed an unpardonable sin.

Much later, after the nuns told her father of her "irreverent, hostile and uncooperative" attitude, he beat her so hard that "her period, which wasn't due for two or three days [was] brought on early by fear and blows." As she recalled, "I looked down and noticed my stockings were covered with blood." Even her mother had to stand by helplessly during such assaults on her children for, besides being psychologically ill-equipped to stand up to authority, her small frame was no match for her husband's strength. On one occasion, when she was trying to comfort her crying baby, he followed her to the bedroom and hurled them both down the stairs. Once, however, Claire's mother did rebel against this brutal treatment. She waited until her husband was sent away on an assignment, then moved her four children home to her parents for the next two years – the only happy time in Claire's childhood. But plagued by guilt for deserting her husband and threatened by the curé with stories of her "duty" to her husband and God, she consented to return to him, knowing full well that he would never keep his promise to reform.

At times Claire "wished her father would die." But her mother chastized her young daughter telling her she must "never wish for anyone's death, least of all [her] father's." Unlike her mother, Claire continued to nurture a consuming hatred for the man who "never put aside his anger [which] was the only thing he really liked." Claire blamed all her father's shortcomings on his anger for she noticed that the success of his rages inspired a kind of desperate pride in him. "Pride engendered egotism; egotism...avarice...avarice...lack of sociability." He was also, in Claire's opinion at least, obsessed with sex which "he thought about incessantly...in the wrong way."

The Church fostered this attitude towards sex which was depicted as "dirty" and "sheer buffoonery." "Procreation alone could save and excuse this abomination." Nevertheless, men could not rid themselves of their physical desires, and since the Church was male-dominated, it blamed women for their unholy lust. In Quebec "all women were disposed to become sluts and a man, even a paragon of virtue, [was] plunged into an abyss of desire by the mere appearance of a breast." Since Claire's father saw her and her sisters in this way, he consequently felt fully justified in keeping them virtual prisoners for close to twenty years.

From the time she was six until she was sixteen, Claire spent the school year in convents under the watchful eye of the nuns who never allowed their charges to leave the grounds, opened all their mail, restricted their reading material, and encouraged them to tell on each other. During the holidays life was no freer. After his wife's return, her father bought a large rambling house in an isolated spot near Quebec City. Not only was there no road to it but it was a fifteen-minute walk to the nearest neighbour. Even communication by mail was limited, as her father forbade Claire to write anyone without first asking his permission.

Claire would have been able to tolerate the isolation if only life around the house had not been so gloomy. "Laughter was forbidden," she wrote, "[since] he never took [it] for anything but a symptom of lewdness." Even toys were forbidden. All but the bare necessities of life were considered frivolous, and even the most natural acts of youth were viewed with mistrust. Claire and her sisters were forbidden to run and shout or to "stray even the slightest distance away from the house."

The death of her mother from tuberculosis when Claire was only thirteen, did nothing to ease this joyless atmosphere. Although this frail, timid woman had never been able to intercede on her children's behalf or save them from her husband's violent rages, she had always been there to comfort and take care of them. Later Claire remembered vividly the days immediately following her mother's death: the train ride to Quebec to her grandparents' home where her mother was laid out for two days; the spectacle of the seven children seated about their mother's coffin, "dry-eyed – frozen stiff by the fear of showing some weakness they would be called upon to account for later on to their father"; her father's constant scolding about petty details; and the sight of her dead mother's face. Only years afterwards did Claire learn that her mother had spent her last days worrying about what would become of her children, especially Claire, "the one who loves her father least."

Back at the convent, life was more miserable then ever for Claire following her mother's death. But then misery was something she had grown to expect from convent life: "When I look back at those wretched years," she wrote later, "I realize that the thing that was lacking in our convents was kindness." Claire had not boarded at the first convent for long when she learned that the Sisters seemed to take great delight in punishing their weaker charges. One day the girls who had not done well in catechism were ordered up to the dormitory and told to take off their dresses. Then one Sister, armed with a stiff brush, scrubbed their faces with laundry soap. "It was a powerful detergent; even without a brush it left the skin raw in no time flat," Claire recalled. "The blondes...came through the ordeal [with] their faces peeling and oozing blood."

Although their physical punishments were harsh, the psychological effects of the Sisters' treatment was far more damaging. They had various "pets" among the girls who, Claire was to learn from experience, acted as informers. One such girl seduced Claire into showing her how her boyfriend kissed her. The next day Claire was called into the Mother Superior's office to find her father waiting. She had been expelled for "doing things with one of her companions." Only her long practice at lying saved her from a beating on this occasion. "The Sisters hate me because you have never made a donation to the convent," she told her father. This won him to her side as she had calculated, for, as everyone knew, he begrudged every cent he spent. Later, he refused to pay the registration fee for Claire's final examinations because, as he would never allow her to work, she would not need a diploma.

He refused to let any of his daughters work as he was afraid of the bad influences they would encounter. "Do you realize," he used to tell Claire, "those girls work all day long surrounded by men?" And Claire knew that "he really believed working girls have every reason in the world to find themselves pregnant after two weeks."

By the time she reached her late teens, Claire admitted she could laugh at such attitudes, but as a young girl she was deeply affected by them. In those days, she used to lash out against the injustices in her life. In time, she learned that this reaction was futile and she withdrew into a fabricated world of lies and fantasy that could not be affected by the cruelties and injustices of her daily life.

She succeeded in isolating herself so well that she could not even take comfort from her brothers and sisters: "Their sympathy didn't move me. Nothing could...I was dried up, completely callous." Instead of fostering a love of God, Claire's upbringing had the opposite effect. "I was not born devout and nothing had occurred in my short life to persuade me that I should have been so...Mother's piety seemed to have very poor returns, my father's was a caricature...Mother Saint-Cheribin's brand was completely mad."

Claire's consuming hatred of her father remained the most lasting effect of her upbringing. In her autobiography, *In an Iron Glove*, she could not bring herself even to mention his name, and despite her protestations that she has "forgiven everything," one constantly comes across traces of her dislike and bitterness towards him in her writing. For one thing, her father's treatment warped her relationship with men for many years. He soon realized that if he could not send his daughters into a convent, he would have to marry them off or be left with five to support. After an unsuccessful attempt to talk his eldest daughter into entering a convent, he began to bring home suitable young men as possible husbands. His daughters, not particularly liking his choice, began to conspire with friends and managed to meet people of their own choice. But in Claire's case, it did not mean that she liked these any better than those her father brought home. She confessed that as a young girl she hated them all. To her, man was the enemy "who could use his superior strength to reduce woman to slavery, beat her, prevent her from doing what she wants." But Claire still dreamed of marriage as a means of escape – and revenge. "Deep inside me there was an unacknowledged and quite wicked plan to make any husband that came my way pay for the whole race...If I'd married young I'd have done what I intended. As luck would have it, I married at thirty-one" by which time she had matured sufficiently to discard such plans.

Shortly after she left the convent at sixteen, an incident in a restaurant made Claire begin to realize how ignorant she was. "One day when I was having lunch in a restaurant in Quebec, two men were talking at the next table. I heard them well enough, but I didn't understand what they were saying...Sometimes they would mention a writer and titles of his works; titles and names were equally unknown to me." Shortly after this incident, Claire went into a bookstore and looked through some of the books they had mentioned, only to find that she understood nothing. "After ten years of study with the nuns, who thought of nothing else but to make us obey, obey, obey, to break in our characters...to make us servile, pious, resigned and prudish" she had learned very little.

Claire found it very difficult to broaden her horizons, for her father made sure that his daughters did not have access to books that might give them new ideas. Claire managed to borrow books from her friends and hid them under her mattress. She knew her father was afraid to comment on her mattress, which was "a mass of bumps and hollows," for fear of having to buy a new one.

Gradually over the years Claire and her brothers and sisters managed – by lying and conspiring – to attain a measure of freedom for themselves. The sisters lied indiscriminately to escape from the isolation their father imposed on them. On one occasion, one of Claire's sisters managed to attend a gala ball by asking her father permission to spend three days in the retreat house. But their hard-won freedom was short-lived, for they unexpectedly found themselves with a stepmother. Claire described her father's new wife as a "fat, grasping, selfish, cold and cruel woman" who stole her stepdaughters' belongings to send to her own daughter. But by this stage in their lives, Claire and her brothers and sisters had been toughened by years of dealing with their father and were determined to fight back. "Before spring had come, open war had been declared between us," and continued to be waged for many years.

In October 1934, Claire's oldest sister married. Although she had known of her sister's romance for months, Claire was surprised, never having believed that any of them would marry and escape their home. Only later did she discover a wedding march is not always the music of liberty.

In time, Claire went on to marry for love, and to find the intellectual fulfilment denied her in her youth. Although a late-starter, she became one of French Canada's outstanding writers with the publication of her two novels *Doux-Amer* (1960) and *Quand j'aurai paye ton visage* (1962) and a volume of short stories *Avec ou sans amour.* In 1965 she published her autobiography *In an Iron Glove* which, ironically, won her the Governor General's award for fiction. Although Claire Martin dwells on the grotesque elements in her childhood, what she has to say is fact, not fiction. The events she described give us a fairly accurate picture of the kind of life that most women and young girls had to endure in Quebec in the first half of the century.

Claire Martin's autobiography did much to show other women in Quebec that their frustrations with their narrow lives were not unique, and her personal success, achieved in spite of her rigid upbringing, offered hope to thousands of her sex.

Thérèse Casgrain

While Claire Martin was growing up, there were a few outstanding women already working for women's rights in Quebec. Thérèse Casgrain was one of their leaders. She was, among other things, the first woman in the province to run in a federal election, the first woman in Canada to serve as provincial leader of a recognized political party, and the first woman in the province to be appointed to the Senate. Her name is familiar to many Canadians, but few people see her achievement against the facts of her background.

Born in Montreal in 1896, Thérèse was the oldest child of one of Quebec's oldest aristocratic French Canadian families. Her father, Rodolphe Forget, who had been knighted in 1912, was a member of the House of Commons from 1904 to 1917 and a stockbroker who gained national prominence by pushing his firm to the top of the Canadian financial world. Powerful, aggressive, and dynamic, he filled his mansion in Montreal and his luxurious summer home at Murray Bay with dignitaries from Canada and abroad, creating the stimulating atmosphere in which his daughter developed her life-long interest in public affairs. Although surrounded by men of power and action, Thérèse was most impressed by her dynamic father. "More than anyone else my father had a dominant influence in my life," she stated more than once. "He was always on the side of the underdog [not] just our servants [but] the working class."

Like other French-Canadian girls from similar backgrounds, Thérèse was educated at a convent and, after her graduation, spent her days shopping, going to parties, and now and then attending a play carefully selected by her parents. As a teenager she was discouraged from taking any steps that might equip her for anything more ambitious than the traditional home-oriented role. She did not even receive any encouragement from her father who, for all his sophistication and intelligence, still adhered to the traditional view of women's role in society. When his daughter, who had always been a good student, asked to continue her education beyond high school, he told her laughingly to "see if the cook can teach you something." In those days Thérèse did not feel the need to rebel and was happy and contented in the role assigned her by birth and sex. At twenty she fell in love with and married Pierre Casgrain, a struggling law student ten years her senior, and for the next few years enjoyed being "in a place of my own" on Montreal's then fashionable Bishop Street, totally absorbed in the role of wife and hostess. Although she had been married only a year when her husband ran as a Liberal in the federal election of 1917 and won the seat in her father's former riding of Charlevoix, Thérèse adjusted easily to the role of politician's wife. And when the couple moved to Ottawa shortly afterwards, her upbringing as a politician's daughter, combined with her innate vivaciousness and curiosity, soon made her a valuable social asset to her husband.

It was not until Pierre Casgrain's second political campaign that Thérèse stepped outside the conventional role as the wife of a public figure. One night during her husband's second campaign, he was taken ill and was unable to appear at an important political rally. His harassed campaign manager thought of the bright, attractive Thérèse and urged her "to offer her husband's excuses" to the audience. She had never made a speech in public before, and now she was asked to address a political audience in a province where a woman's involvement in politics was inconceivable, but she agreed. The speech was a success, and, soon after she returned to Montreal, a few women's right supporters invited her to join their efforts to form a bilingual provincial suffrage association. Their aim was to convince the public and members of the legislature that women's suffrage could be of social advantage to the province.

In 1922 the Comité provincial pour le Suffrage féminin was born. It was as a member of the Comité that Thérèse first encountered anti-feminist abuse. When a 400-member delegation went to Quebec to ask the government to grant the vote to women, Mme Casgrain pointed out to the Premier, who had received the group in the dining room of the Legislature, that "the place he had chosen was quite in harmony with the viewpoint of [the Legislature] since it was next to the kitchen, the place to which ladies are generally relegated." This sort of treatment was to prove comparatively mild and Premier Taschereau but one of many obstacles in the struggle for women's suffrage in Quebec. The Church was, of course, one of the strongest adversaries and, because the clergy "generally-speaking were opposed to votes for women, they were largely responsible for perpetrating women's backward and subservient position in Quebec society." Moreover, what did not get said in the pulpit got said in the newspapers. The papers were full of letters outlining the clergy's views on women's suffrage, letters such as that of L.N. Cardinal Begin, published in 1932, which stated that "the entry of women into politics, even by merely voting, would be a misfortune for our province. Nothing justifies it, neither the natural law nor the good of society." Frequent church bulletins to this effect made submission to the established authority "de riguer – whether among the clergy or in governments or in society in general." Even liberal thinkers felt obliged to curb any progressive opinions in deference to the Church. L. Perrin, curé of Nôtre-Dame, tempered his ardent plea for women's suffrage with this statement;

> Is it advisable at the present moment for Canadian women of the Catholic faith to concern themselves with political questions? The only authority competent to answer this question is that of our bishops, whose duty it is to direct us and to whose authority it is sweet and easy for us to submit, knowing the heavy burden they are required at times to bear and the anguish that often fills their hearts.

In view of this opposition, the well-known feminist, Mme Gérin-Lajoie, resigned as president of the Comité provincial pour le Suffrage féminin. Mme Casgrain had no doubt at the time that her colleague was "yielding to strong pressure from the Bishops of Quebec." She herself, however, was not about to tolerate interference from the Church, and at a time when most Catholic associations had their own chaplains, she defied tradition by deciding not to have a chaplain associated with the Ligue de la Jeunesse Féminine, a French-Canadian Junior League that she had organized in 1926. "Such an appointment was unnecessary since our members had already received the upbringing they required to meet their responsibilities," she argued in answer to those who considered the Ligue's position scandalous.

In this case Mme Casgrain met with great success, but many of her efforts, especially those in the area of women's rights, proved ineffectual and slow to bear fruit. The Comité's lack of progress was the underlying reason for a split among its members in 1927. At that time some members decided to break away, a move that Thérèse thought did "considerable damage [by] delighting [their] enemies." In spite of such temporary setbacks Thérèse felt generally encouraged by the results of her work: "The public was beginning to accept our ideas and several women's groups that had engaged till then only in charitable work began to support the efforts of our committee," she recalls. In an effort to gain even more publicity for its platform and to influence public opinion in 1927, the Comité decided to introduce a bill in favour of female suffrage at every session of the Legislature. Thérèse had argued vehemently in favour of this move although many Comité members considered it "a useless gesture since the Prime Minister and the leader of the Opposition were still of one mind in their opposition to such a bill."

When Victor Marchand, a member of the Legislative Assembly, introduced the controversial bill, it was defeated by a vote of fifty-one to thirteen. Nonetheless, Mme Casgrain and her group were determined to reintroduce the issue time and time again. This determination needed considerable personal courage for "often certain members even went so far as to reply to our requests with jeers, vulgarities or cutting remarks before bringing down their verdicts of curt rejection." Mme Casgrain, who was president of the Ligue for fourteen years, was a prime target for such jibes.

As president of the Ligue, Mme Casgrain became a prominent figure not only in Quebec but across the country, for she was a frequent and popular speaker on the status of women in Quebec. She was also the director of a weekly radio show sponsored by the Ligue, in which sketches illustrated the laws of Quebec and how they affected women. She had once told a Toronto reporter that "as far as women's suffrage is concerned, we are not going to go back begging it of the Legislature any more. We are going to mobilize public opinion...through the radio...by which we can reach the women in their homes all over the province."

Through her radio show and public addresses, Mme Casgrain gradually won support for her cause. Following one of her speeches in Toronto, one of the city's daily papers published an editorial pointing out the archaic laws that kept women from serving on the school board, or the minimum wage board, or any public agency that dealt with the interests of women, children, and the home. Newspaper accounts of Mme Casgrain's speeches usually included comments about her appearance for reporters were surprised that this energetic suffragette was a chic, blue-eyed beauty whose good looks and flair for fashion caught many an eye. As one reporter put it, "she had a beautiful face and head set off by the smartest hat I've yet seen."

Attractive, charming, and of good social standing, Thérèse Casgrain did not hesitate to use these assets in the fight for women's rights in Quebec. As she readily admitted, "I was able to make valuable political contacts that greatly aided our cause." Equally important for a women's rights worker at that time, was her image as wife and mother, which did much to destroy the stereotype picture of the suffragette as a "plain-looking spinster...if not [a] lesbian." With her quick wits and good sense of humour, she often laughed at some of the bizarre situations that resulted from Quebec's archaic laws. In 1935, there was a federal election one month and a Quebec provincial election the next. "We organized and the men treated us very well indeed," she recalls. "We had teas, meetings, speakers and everything. Then when the provincial election came along a month later, [the men] kept asking us, 'Why don't you leave us alone?' 'Why don't you run along home?' " While she could laugh at the irony of it, Mme Casgrain was also quick to point out to her friends "that won't happen when we get the provincial vote."

Mme Casgrain's sense of humour and her non-militant approach, which contrasted with the extreme measures advocated by some feminists, won her a degree of admiration, if not support, from her adversaries. As she said, "It is always harder to catch flies with vinegar than with honey." In this spirit, Ligue members arranged for a bouquet of sixty-three red roses to be placed on Premier Taschereau's desk on the occasion of his sixty-third birthday, in a gesture to show they were above being petty. Thérèse felt that it was important to keep the lines of communication open if feminists hoped to accomplish anything. And, as the letter from the Premier showed, she had succeeded in this case. "You are 'a good sport' and I do not deserve the flowers," he wrote. "I should like to congratulate you on your personal success. You have opened a breach in our ranks which we shall now have to repair." This was not the only time Mme Casgrain used such tactics in handling the Premier who had once joked that in the unlikely event that she, a leading suffragette, should have another child, he would like to be the godfather. When Mme Casgrain did give birth to her fourth child, she reminded the Premier of his offer which he honoured. They remained friends privately, even though they continued to fight publicly.

Mme Casgrain's position as the wife of a prominent Liberal and Speaker of the House was both a "blessing and a curse." On the one hand, she had easy access to powerful people, but on the other, she was more often singled out as the target for anti-feminist attacks. Once when emptying her husband's pockets she came across a cartoon showing a man beating his wife. On it the anonymous sender had written, "That's what you should do to yours." Well aware that her husband had to put up with a constant stream of such abuse, Thérèse Casgrain was always grateful to him for giving her the freedom to act according to her principles. "He was the type of man who didn't object to his wife becoming somebody. That takes a big man."

Pierre Casgrain was a "big man" in his own right in public life and had little cause to be jealous of his wife's accomplishments. He was the member of Parliament for the riding of Charlevoix-Saguenay for twenty-four years, during which time he served as Liberal whip, Speaker of the House of Commons, and Secretary of State. He also became one of the leading members of the Montreal bar and was eventually appointed to the Quebec Superior Court in 1941. Thérèse had followed her husband's activities with interest and he reciprocated in his support, concern, and advice for her projects and struggles. But an even greater bond lay in their enjoyment of family life. Pierre, who had lost his mother when he was only three and had been raised by his grandmother, had always looked forward to having a home of his own.

In 1936, the reactionary Taschereau government fell and was succeeded by Maurice Duplessis and the Union Nationale. The change in leadership brought few advantages for women, as anti-feminism continued to flourish as strongly as ever. It soon became apparent that Duplessis opposed women's suffrage as violently as his predecessor. "I sat opposite Taschereau for ten years. I learned his methods; in fact I've improved on them," Duplessis once told Mme Casgrain. Thérèse saw one good result of Duplessis' anti-feminism stand; it rekindled the Ligue members' lagging interest in the struggle for women's rights. When Mackenzie King appointed the Rowell-Sirois Commission in August 1937 to look into the whole question of federal and provincial jurisdiction and tax sharing, the Ligue asked Miss Elizabeth Monk, an eminent Quebec attorney, to prepare a brief for submission to the commission. While the brief brought little immediate success, Thérèse Casgrain felt that it at least "focused [the] attention of the Federal Government on the appalling status of women in her province." Because of Duplessis' blatant anti-feminist views, the Ligue supported the Liberals in the provincial election of 1939 as women's suffrage was part of the party program. Whether this influenced the outcome of the provincial election is difficult to determine, but Duplessis and the Union Nationale were defeated.

Mme Casgrain's rekindled hopes were short-lived however. Months passed and the new Liberal and supposedly pro-feminist Premier Adélard Godbout made no reference to the question of women's suffrage. Mme Casgrain called on all interested women to remind him of his promise at the convention. At last, in February 1940, the Women's Suffrage Bill was included in the speech from the throne, sparking a new series of attacks from reactionary Quebequers, especially the clergy. An article in the influential *La Semaine Réligieuse* left no doubt where the Catholic Church in Quebec stood on the question of women's suffrage. "We are not in favour of female political suffrage [because it is] contrary to the unity and authority structure of the family...It exposes women to all the passions and intrigues of electoralism...Women of the province don't really want it...reform could be just as well achieved through the influence of female organizations outside politics." Premier Godbout, a good Catholic, was surprised by the narrow-mindedness of the Church's position and informed Cardinal Villeneuve that he had no intention of remaining at his post if the Church's opposition to the vote for women did not cease. He threatened to resign and ask the Lieutenant Governor in Council to call the Honourable T.D. Bouchard to form a new government. Since Bouchard's anti-clerical views were well known, the Church's objections to the bill stopped abruptly.

In April 1941, after a twenty-year struggle, Mme Casgrain watched Premier Adélard Godbout introduce Bill No. 18 in the Legislative Assembly granting the women of Quebec the right to vote in provincial elections.

But Thérèse Casgrain's hopes for a new era in Quebec were

premature. Having obtained the vote, Quebec women seemed unwilling to fight for the numerous rights still denied them. Under Quebec law, a woman became her husband's chattel through marriage; she had no authority over her own body, her children, or her own property. Without her husband's consent, a woman could not have a surgical operation, even to save her own life. A married woman had no legal right over her own wages even though some 160,000 Quebec women were in the work force. Even the property she inherited or purchased herself could not be disposed of without her husband's consent. With these and many other injustices still in existence, it was clear to Thérèse that her work was far from finished.

She became involved in numerous organizations, many of which she was instrumental in forming. Over the years, these organizations, some of which were national and international in scope, including the League for Human Rights, the Consultive Committee and the Administration of Justice in Quebec, worked to secure and protect individual rights. In time, however, Thérèse Casgrain became convinced that all effective reform rested with the government, and that if she wanted to be an effective reformer she would have to be elected to Parliament. By the time she had reached this conclusion, conditions in her life had altered enough to allow her to seek public office. Her husband had been appointed to the Montreal Superior Court in 1942, her children were almost grown-up, and her most time-consuming job – the struggle for women's franchise – was over and won.

In November 1942, a seat fell vacant in Charlevoix-Saguenay – the riding represented by her father as a Conservative and later by her husband as a Liberal. Thérèse decided to run as an Independent Liberal, but despite a long and strenuous campaign, she came second out of the five candidates, losing to the Liberal, Frederic Dorion. She was defeated mainly because she refused to compromise or toe the party line. She spoke out against conscription at a time when Liberal Prime Minister Mackenzie King was trying to get French Canadians to accept it. As Mme Casgrain pointed out, "the Liberals had opposed this measure in all their election campaigns of the previous twenty-five years and had condemned the Conservative Mr. Borden for bringing in conscription against the wishes of the French Canadians during World War I. And now, these self-same Liberals were trying to get the measure accepted by our people, on the insistence of their leader, Mr. King and others of his cabinet. After all that had been said on this matter, it is easy to understand the resistance of the population." She also opposed what were known as "cash grants" to England – funds lent to the Churchill Government for the war. Although she believed strongly in the need for Canada to help and urged French Canadians to volunteer their services, Mme Casgrain was branded an enemy of the people and lost much public support. Moreover, so as not to displease the federal Liberals, Premier Godbout did not support any of the three Independent Liberal candidates seeking election in the riding.

Despite her defeat, Mme Casgrain did not give up the idea of a political career. In December 1946, she created somewhat of a scandal by officially joining the c.c.f. Party. As the daughter of a well-known and wealthy Conservative and the wife of an equally well-known Liberal, former Speaker of the House of Commons, and former Secretary of State in Mackenzie King's cabinet and current Judge of the Quebec Superior Court, Thérèse Casgrain's latest move caused what she described as "a stir" in social and political circles. Unfortunately, most of the embarrassment fell on Pierre Casgrain, although he had agreed with her decision. "I made my career in the Liberal party," he told her, "but I can very well understand that you might take a different road." Reporters and public alike were surprised that someone from Mme Casgrain's social class and background would join a socialist party, but she explained that "Many years ago, I came to the conclusion that the old parties would not work for the benefit of the average citizen. I made up my mind that the c.c.f. platform comes closest to what I believe in for the social and economic welfare of the people."

Mme Casgrain encountered many difficulties while working for the c.c.f., a party that was under attack from those in power. They were constantly without election funds and constantly battling against public opinion. She spent a great deal of her time at meetings and conventions where her training and abilities as a committee woman were soon recognized. At the National Convention in Winnipeg in 1948, she was elected in absentia as a vice-president of the c.c.f. Her election confirmed her belief that the c.c.f. had no prejudice against women, and also allowed her to become the principal spokesman for the French Canadians in the c.c.f. The task proved to be the most difficult and most thankless of her career. Thérèse knew from experience that it was difficult to get new ideas accepted in Quebec, but the job of selling the c.c.f. platform was next to impossible. Not only were French Canadians justifiably suspicious of a party whose English-speaking members frequently showed great ignorance and prejudice on the subject of Quebec and the rights of the French, but whose basic tenets were completely contrary to prevailing attitudes in Quebec.

Thérèse Casgrain had just begun to work on this challenge when her husband died suddenly in August 1950 at the age of sixty-four. As a widow, Mme Casgrain threw herself more than ever into politics. In 1952 she ran unsuccessfully on the c.c.f. ticket in Verdun. Despite her defeat, she ran again the same year in a by-election in Outremont-Saint-Jean. Once again, she was defeated. Then, in 1953, she ran in Jacques-Cartier-Lasalle and met her third defeat in two years. Reporters branded her "a misfit" who "as a Liberal or even a Conservative in French Canada...would probably win an election...but as a c.c.f. candidate [would go] down to defeat every time." This, to at least one reporter, was a decided loss to Canadian public life.

Despite her failure to win a seat in Parliament, Mme Casgrain worked hard to make the c.c.f. a more viable and effective political party for Canadians. In 1955, the provincial branch of the party changed its name to Le Parti Social Democratique du Quebec in an effort to communicate its aims to voters, and Mme Casgrain was re-elected provincial leader. But when in the federal election in March 1958 the c.c.f. won only eight seats, the lowest figure since 1940, members of the party were forced to realize that it must become a more broadly based political movement that could embrace all liberal-minded people interested in basic social reform and reconstruction through the parliamentary system of government. By 1961, this had resulted in the formation of the New Democratic Party.

Although sixty-five years old, Thérèse Casgrain was elected to the national council of the N.D.P. and remained involved with party policy on a national level. The various provinces soon formed their own branches of the N.D.P., but here again, as in most movements that advocated change at that time, Quebec lagged behind the rest of Canada. Considering her four defeats at the polls, it took great optimism and determination for Thérèse Casgrain to wage her fifth political campaign. As she once confessed to columnist Margaret Aitken, if she could have "but one session in the Parliament of Canada, but one session, [she] would die happy."

In 1963, at the age of sixty-seven, Mme Casgrain became so incensed at Opposition Leader Lester Pearson's suggestion that the Conservative government should accept nuclear warheads as defensive weapons, that she offered herself as "a candidate for peace." The Minister of Justice at the time, Pierre Elliot Trudeau, made a speech on her behalf on that occasion as he, too, strongly opposed Canada's acceptance of nuclear weapons. Despite this support, Thérèse Casgrain lost again. Her only consolation was that the victorious Liberals could only form a minority government.

In 1970, Mme Casgrain received a phone call from Prime Minister Pierre Trudeau, an old family friend and former supporter, offering her a seat in the Senate. He told her to consider it but she immediately accepted thinking that "if I take some time he'll think I'm going to ask some man." Although the Prime Minister was criticized for trying to woo western socialists through her and other non-Liberal appointments, no one could deny that Senator Casgrain had earned her seat in the Senate. On October 8, 1970, Thérèse Casgrain was sworn in as Senator at the age of seventy-four.

The new Senator soon turned to issues involving the status

of women and attempted to direct public attention to the unjust laws governing women in Quebec. As Senator Casgrain pointed out, Quebec women were still not eligible to serve on juries – a right women possessed in all other provinces except Newfoundland. "To my great satisfaction," she recalls, "a bill was introduced in Newfoundland a few weeks later, putting an end to this discrimination; Quebec followed suit in May 1971." When the Royal Commission on the Status of Women in Canada was tabled in the Senate in December 1970, she objected to it on the grounds that it offered no constructive criticism. "The facts in the report...are all the more disturbing since they are the result of objective and non-ideological analysis. They only confirm what everyone has long known about the discrimination women face."

On July 10, 1971 Mme Casgrain reached the age of seventy-five, the age of compulsory retirement from the Senate. And so after only nine months, she reluctantly left the Senate. During that brief period as Senator, she had at last been given the opportunity to prove her theory that all effective reform lies with the government. "Placed at the heart of the parliament of my country I had felt that I was working with far more authority and effectiveness. My opinions had finally become respectable for they were those of a senator. Yet I was neither more intelligent nor more dynamic than before."

Today, Thérèse Casgrain still takes a keen interest in the struggle for individual rights. "All my life I have recommended that one must ask questions, take a position, and act upon it," she says. She approves in general of the wave of women's liberation that is spreading over the world, though she differs with some of the methods a few groups use to attain their goals. "Our case is surely not strengthened because some thousands of them throw, if not all sense of propriety to the wind, at least their bras into the fire," she said recently. At a time when the women's movement often lacks both wit and humour, Thérèse Casgrain still possesses an abundance of both.

Epilogue

In the century from 1840 to 1940, most of the major battles for women's rights in this country were fought and won. Because of the work of suffragettes such as Emily Stowe, Nellie McClung, and Emily Murphy, women are now eligible to vote in federal and provincial elections. In the famous "Persons Case" of 1929, the "five women from Alberta" fought for the Canadian woman's right to be appointed to the Senate. The successful campaigns for reform legislation, waged by women such as Helen MacGill and Emily Murphy, meant that women no longer give up rights to their property when they marry and are entitled to a portion of the estate if their husband dies before them. Moreover, due to the persistence and fortitude of Augusta Stowe-Gullen, Helen MacGill, Clara Brett Martin, and Martha Hamm Lewis, among others, women today are admitted to universities, teachers' colleges, and the professions.

But, despite these encouraging signs of change, age-old prejudices and customs have not been uprooted quickly or easily. Faced with negative reactionary attitudes and fear, Nellie McClung, Emily Stowe, Emily Murphy, Adelaide Hoodless, and Helen MacGill recognized that they must educate the public, and especially women, to the need for women's franchise. Without the vote, they knew they had little power to effect any reform legislation. In countries like New Zealand, the Scandinavian countries, and several American states, women's suffrage had been quickly followed by changes in the laws especially in those areas concerning women and children.

The Canadian suffragettes were determined to show women that they must do something to help themselves. "Women have wept and waited too long," argued Nellie McClung. "Human justice does not come ready-made, we have to fight for it."

Most of these crusaders for change saw women's groups as one of the most effective means of propagating new ideas. Adelaide Hoodless launched her crusade to teach domestic science through the Hamilton Y, and Helen MacGill, an inveterate "joiner" all her life, directly attributed Quebec women's failure to win any rights to their lack of organization. Significantly the development of Canadian women's rights' groups was patterned in part on the groups already formed in the United States and England. For example, Emily Stowe formed the Women's Literary Guild in Toronto in 1877 after attending a meeting in Cleveland of the American Society for the Advancement of Women.

These early feminists also tried to educate the public by a variety of other methods. Helen MacGill wrote a booklet on laws regarding women and children which she had published at her own expense and sold for twenty-five cents. In 1896 in Toronto, members of the Women's Christian Temperance Union organized a mock parliament, called the Ontario Legislature of Women, in an effort to advertise their reasons for wanting provincial franchise. It proved so successful that suffragettes in Winnipeg borrowed the idea and staged their own highly successful mock parliament in 1914 to point up the reactionary views of the anti-feminist Conservative government, which persisted in denying them the provincial franchise.

Nellie McClung also used her writing as a vehicle for her social criticism. In a blatant attempt to tell women how they could help themselves among other things, Mrs. McClung created heroines who fought against tremendous odds for a better life, which they always succeeded in attaining.

While many of these pioneers struggled for women's rights and fought to dispel anti-feminist myths through education, others influenced women by their individual struggles for satisfying lives. Their unconventional lifestyles and their success in their respective fields across the country helped to win over public opinion. In fact, whether they were aware of it or not, all these nineteenth-century pioneers contributed in one way or another to debunk Victorian myths about women. Kit Coleman, for instance, defying the advice of her editors at the *Mail and Empire*, wangled a passage to Cuba to cover the Spanish-American War in 1898 and, in the process, disproved their fears that "a woman couldn't stand the pace, the hours or the language." By successfully running a mill near Dawson City in the 1890's, Martha Black surprised those who had predicted that a lady could not survive alone in the North. Ma Murray's tenacious and outrageous career as British Columbia's newspaper gadfly won her fame and often notoriety. By distinguishing themselves academically at university, Helen MacGill and Maude Abbott did much to debunk the anti-feminists' contention that women were "tremulous creatures, incapable of concentrated study and given to fits of the vapours under pressure." Moreover, the fact that Maude Abbott and Cora Hind both achieved international recognition in their respective fields of medicine and journalism proved that a woman could have as much to offer society intellectually as a man.

These women shared one thing in common, whether they became avid supporters of women's rights or strove by excellence to set an example for others: their concern with the question began when they found their own plans thwarted by prejudice against their sex.

In the Canadian scene today, women are now at home in many of the professions that were strictly male territory in the nineteenth century – teaching, medicine, journalism, architecture, engineering, and law. However, within these professions, they are kept within the boundaries that, though not as rigidly defined as in the nineteenth century, are nevertheless very much in existence. The majority of women never reach positions of major responsibility or power. There are countless female teachers, lecturers, and professors, but few female university deans or presidents. There are many women journalists, reporters, and editors, but not many become editors-in-chief of large metropolitan dailies. There are almost as many women as men in the business world, but far fewer proportionately are managers, directors or board members.

In the field of politics, of the 264 members in the House of Commons, only nine are women. In fact, since Agnes Macphail became the first woman M.P. in 1921, only twenty-seven women have served in the Canadian House of Commons, and of these, few have distinguished themselves apart from making headlines for being women in a man's world.

In the Senate, women have fared no better. Following the long and by now famous "Person's Case" resulting in the Privy Council's ruling in October 1929 that made Canadian women eligible for appointment to the Senate, one might have expected more women senators. However, since Cairine Wilson became the first woman senator in Canada in 1931, only fourteen out of the 102 members have been women.

Why is the way ahead so difficult, so slow?

In the nineteenth century, women were held back, both by disparity in educational opportunities and by social pressures to conform to expected roles. But now, since the physical barriers have been removed to a large extent, there must be other pressures working to keep women from occupying positions of power and responsibility.

There are a number of reasons why this movement has been so long in the offing. First, there was so little overlap from victory to victory; the triumps were short-lived. Consequently, the battle had to be fought again and again, both as women strove to penetrate different professions and as they did so in different parts of the country. Secondly, the persistence of role expectation has been responsible for snuffing out women's initiative and barring them from achievement. From early childhood, boys and girls are sex-typed – in their toys, parental expectations and education – and these expectations have been unconsciously incorporated into their own approach to life.

Of course, these traditional expectations have to a degree been changed and overcome. There is more encouragement for women to work and to step outside the prescribed paths. One-third of the labour force is now composed of women; married women comprise thirty five per cent of female workers. However, the concept of a woman as having a right to be economically independent with interests outside the domestic sphere, (as opposed to a "protected," dependent wife and mother) is still far from universal. Hence, she is less often considered for advancement and responsibility; indeed, she less often sees herself as pursuing such a course.

Finally, significant change in women's lot undermines the power structure of our society. Since a revolution in attitudes and values invariably threatens institutions and lifestyles – marriage, the family, the balance of power between the sexes – one can see why any change as significant as that of women's role in society is bound to be slow and fraught with obstacles.

Notes

CHAPTER ONE

page	line	source
14	19-21	Louis Tivy, *Your Loving Anna*, p. 91.
14	24-27	*Ibid.*, p.48.
14	30-31	*Ibid.*, p.26
15	23-26	C. A. Carter and T. M. Bailey (eds.), *The Diary of Sophia Macnab*, p. 43.
15	33ff	Martha Black, *My Seventy Years*, pp. 53-54.
16	10-14	*Ibid.*, p. 49.
16	31-33	Rev. Robert Wilson, *Piety Portrayed in the lives of Mr. and Mrs. Burpee*, no pages given.
17	13-22	C. E. Phillips, *The Development of Education in Canada*, p. 379.
17	31	Carter and Bailey, *The Diary of Sophia Macnab*, p.29.
17	35-37	Mollie Gillen, "Maud Montgomery: the girl who wrote Green Gables," *Chatelaine*, July 1973, p. 40.
18	5-9	S. A. Heward and Wallace, W. S. (eds.), *An American Lady in Old Toronto*, p. 102.

CHAPTER TWO

page	line	source
22	27-28	Rev. George Patterson, *Memoirs of the Rev. S. F. Johnston, the Rev. J. W. Matheson and Mrs. Mary Johnston Matheson, Missionaries of Tanna*, pp. 326-330.
22	30-32	Mrs. Amelia B. Johnson, *A Brief Memoir and Letters of Amelia, Annie and Thomas Johnson*, p. 56.
23	1-7	*Ibid.*, pp. 154-155.
23	19	Ruth Buchanan, *My Mother*, p. 1.
24	2-7	Joyce Marshall, Introduction to *Word from New France: The Selected Letters of Marie de l'Incarnation*, p. 19.

Anna Gaudin

The main sources for the biographical sketch of Anna Gaudin are:
—Samuel Gaudin, *Forty-Four Years with the Northern Cree.*
—Samuel Gaudin, "Letters to the Mission Board."
—Nan Shipley, *Anna and the Indians.*
—Telephone interviews with Mrs. Esther Ross of Transcona, Manitoba, only surviving child of Samuel and Anna Gaudin.
—Interview with the Rev. Dr. J. A. C. Kell, former missionary in northern Manitoba and friend of the Gaudins.
—Telephone interview with Mrs. J. A. C. Kell.

Unless otherwise specified all quotations are taken from *Forty-Four Years with the Northern Cree.* Additional references and extracts are listed below:

page	line	source
26	11-19	Dr. F. J. Shepherd, in Dr. H. E. MacDermot, *The Nursing School of Montreal General Hospital.*
27	30-33	Esther Ross, Telephone interview.
28	16-17	Nan Shipley, *Anna and the Indians,* p. 1.
29	4-7	Samuel Gaudin, *Forty-Four Years with the Northern Cree,* p. 161.
29	16-20	*Ibid.,* p. 57.
29	23-27	*Ibid.,* p. 63.
29	33ff	*Ibid.,* p. 63.
30	7-13	*Ibid.,* p. 65.
30	29	Mrs. J. A. C. Kell, Telephone interview.
31	19-26	Gaudin, *Forty-Four Years with the Northern Cree,* p. 163.
31	30ff	*Ibid.*
32	30-34	Rev. Dr. J. A. C. Kell, Interview.
33	17-18	Ross, Telephone interview.
33	27	Shipley, *Anna and the Indians,* p. 79.
33	32ff	Ross, Interview, December, 1973.
35	6-8	Shipley, *Anna and the Indians,* p. 117.
35	36-37	Ross, Telephone interview.
36	21-28	Edna Kell, *Elizabeth McDougall,* p. 15.
37	5-11, 14-28	Ross, Telephone interview.
37	32-34	Gaudin, *Forty-Four Years with the Northern Cree,* p. 132.
38	5-20	*Ibid.,* p.133.
39	13-16	Gaudin, Letter of Mission Board, July 6, 1907.
40	1-10, 14-22	Gaudin, *Forty-Four Years with the Northern Cree,* p. 168.
40	25-30	Gaudin, Letter to Mission Board, July 1909.
41-42	1ff	Gaudin, *Forty-Four Years with the Northern Cree,* p. 155.
42	15-18	Ross, Interview.
42	23-24	Gaudin, *Forty-Four Years with the Northern Cree,* p. 164.
43	1-4	*Ibid.,* p. 167.
44	11-23	*Ibid.,* p. 165.

CHAPTER THREE

page	line	source
48	31-33	Ellis Lucia, *Klondike Kate,* p. 12.
49	16-18	Martha Black, *My Seventy Years,* pp. 157-158.
50	8-12	*Ibid.,* p. 169.

Peggy Shand

The main source for the biographical portrait of Peggy Shand is Margaret Shand and Ora M. Shand, *The Summit and Beyond.*

Unless otherwise specified, all quotations are from the above source. Additional sources include Pierre Berton, *The Klondike Fever,* and Ellis Lucia, *Klondike Kate.*

page	line	source
53	24-31	Shand and Shand, *The Summit and Beyond,* p. 43.
54	12-21	*Ibid.,* p. 52.
55	15-22	*Ibid.,* p. 43.
58	23-31	*Ibid.,* p. 116.
62	16-23	*Ibid.,* p. 155.
64	26-32	*Ibid.,* p. 300.

Martha Black

The biographical portrait of Martha Black is drawn largely from the following sources:
—Mrs. George Black, *My Seventy Years.*
—Laura Berton, *I Married the Klondike.*
—Jean Johnston, *Wilderness Women.*
—*Hansard,* January 1936 to April 1939.
—Assorted newspaper clippings and conversations with Mrs. James Wyard, Whitehorse.

Unless otherwise specified, statements attributed to Martha Black are taken from *My Seventy Years.*

page	line	source
68	1-11	Black, *My Seventy Years,* pp. 9-10.
69	26-29	"A Canadian Flag," *Hansard,* Vol. I, 1938, p. 430.
70	6-9	Martha Black, *Diary,* February 27, 1937.
70 71	16-19; 32-33	"Woman is Canadian Lawmaker," *Buffalo Evening News,* May 27, 1937.
	28-34	Unidentified news clipping, 1938.

CHAPTER FOUR

page	line	source
88	27-30	Mabel Burkholder, *"Kit": Life of Kathleen Blake Coleman,* pp. 9-11.
88	35-37	*Ibid.,* p. 11.

Margaret Murray

The main source for Margaret Murray's biographical sketch is Georgina Keddell, *The Newspapering Murrays.*

Unless otherwise specified all references to Margaret Murray are taken from the above source (revised 1974 edition). Extracts and additional references are as follows:.

page	line	source
92	20-29	Keddell, *The Newspapering Murrays,* p. 31.
94	10-14	*Ibid.,* p. 74.
95	6-7	Margaret Murray, Telephone interview, February 12, 1974.
95	20	Murray, Telephone interview.
99	10-15	Keddell, *The Newspapering Murrays,* p. 174.
100	15-16	Stephen Franklin, "Ma Murray: Fighting Editor," *Weekend Magazine.*
102	8-9	Jackson House, "Ma Murray: Salty Scourge of Lillooet," *Maclean's Magazine,* pp. 18 and 48.
102	15-16	Margaret Murray, Letter to the author, March 1974.
103	18-21	Keddell, *The Newspapering Murrays,* p. 228.
104	8-17	Reprinted by Scott Young, *The Globe and Mail,* January 9, 1968.
104	31-32	*The Globe and Mail,* April 14, 1973.

CHAPTER FIVE

page	line	source
107	11-19	Elsie MacGill, *My Mother the Judge,* pp. 45-46.
108	15-16	Alice Collins, *Elizabeth Veals,* no page reference.

Helen MacGill

The main sources for Helen MacGill's biography were Elsie MacGill, *My Mother the Judge,* and Elsie MacGill, Interview, Toronto: May, 1973.

Extracts and additional sources are as follows:

page	line	source
110	31ff	Elsie MacGill, Interview.
112	15	University of Toronto opened its doors to women in 1884, but since university federation did not occur until 1904, Trinity was free to decide its stand on this matter for itself.
120	10-14	Helen Gregory MacGill, "Women Have not Failed in Politics," *Liberty Magazine.*
121	35ff	MacGill, *My Mother the Judge,* p. 166.
122	5-7	Elsie MacGill, Interview.
124	6	*Ibid.*
124	30-31	*Ibid.*

CHAPTER SIX

page	line	source
128	3-6	Lorne Pierce in *The Royal Commission on Book Publishing,* p. 27.

128	25-30	Laura Salverson, *Confessions of an Immigrant's Daughter*, p. 413.
129	23-24	*Ibid.*, p. 521.
130	7	Emily Murphy, *Janey Canuck in the West*, p. 138.
130	21-22	McClung, *In Times Like These*, p. 76.
131	34-35	McClung, *The Stream Runs Fast*, p. 64.
131	36-37	McClung, Foreword to *The Next of Kin*, pp. 3,4.

Nellie McClung

The main sources from which this biographical portrait has been drawn are:
Nellie McClung, *Clearing in the West.*
_____. *The Stream Runs Fast.*
_____. *In Times Like These.*
—Eleanor Harman, "Five Persons from Alberta," *The Clear Spirit.*
—Marcia McClung (granddaughter), Interview.

Extracts and additional references are listed below.

132	21-26	McClung, *The Stream Runs Fast*, p. 47.
133	4-7	McClung, *Clearing in the West*, p. 283.
133	25-27	*Ibid.*, p. 298.
134	9ff	McClung, *Clearing in the West*, p. 288.
135	1-3	*Ibid.*, p. 313.
135	11-15	*Ibid.*, p. 309.
135	32-34	McClung, *The Stream Runs Fast*, p. 16.
136	3-9	McClung, *Clearing in the West*, p. 281-2.
136	15-21	McClung, *The Stream Runs Fast*, p. 75.
138	2-6	*Ibid.*, p. 100.
138	16-20	*Ibid.*, p. 105.
138	36ff	*Ibid.*, pp. 108-109.
140	2-3	*Telegram*, Winnipeg, January 29, 1914.
140	27-28	Margaret Zeiman, "Nellie Was a Lady Terror," *Maclean's Magazine.*
141	9	McClung, "The Family Should Not Suffer," Unidentified News Clipping.
141	12-18	*Ibid.*
142	14-15	McClung, *The Stream Runs Fast*, p. 184.
142	23-27	Catherine Cleverdon, *The Women's Suffrage Movement in Canada*, p. 46.
143	5-10	McClung, *The Stream Runs Fast*, p. 173.
143	27-35	*Ibid.*, p. 174.
145	8-17	McClung, *The Stream Runs Fast*, p. 182.

CHAPTER SEVEN

I have based my observations in this chapter largely on information from these sources:
—Augusta Stowe-Gullen, "Stowe Scrapbooks."
—Joanne Thompson, "The Influence of Dr. Emily Stowe on the Woman's Suffrage Movement in Canada," *Ontario History.*
—Carlotta Hacker, *The Indominable Lady Doctors.*

—Byrne Hope Sanders, *Famous Women*.
—Scriver, Jessie Boyd. "Maude E. Abbott" in *The Clear Spirit*.
—Hugh MacDermott, *Maude Abbott. A Memoir*.
—Kennethe M. Haig, *Brave Harvest*.

Extracts and additional sources are as follows:

page	line	source
148	7-9	Mary Bradley, *A Narrative of the Life and Christian Experience of Mrs. Mary Bradley of St. John, N.B.*, p. 83.
148	35ff	Alice Ravenhill, *Memoirs of an Educational Pioneer*, p. 180.
149	27-31	Doris French, *High Button Bootstraps*, p. 19.
150	5-7	C. E. Phillips, *The Development of Education in Canada*, p. 555.
151	3-5;	
	10-11	Byrne Hope Sanders, *Famous Women*, p. 91.
153	6-12	*The Western Law Times*, Volume 2, 1891.
154	11-14	Kennethe Haig, *Brave Harvest*, p. 18.
155	14-17	Superintendent Goggin, *Proceedings*, Dominion Educational Association, (47) 1904, p. 39.
155	19-20	President Burwash as reported by C. E. Phillips in *The Development of Education in Canada*, p. 555.
155	21-23	C. E. Phillips, *The Development of Education in Canada*, p. 555.
156	1-11	*Buffalo Express*, September 1896.
156	24-28	Katherine F. C. MacNaughton. *The Development of the Theory and Practice of Education in New Brunswick*, p. 140.
156	33ff	*Historical Sketch of Medical Education of Women in Kingston*. Paper read before the Osler Club, Queen's University, September 14, 1916.
157	11-15	Haig, *Brave Harvest*, p. 246.
158	31-32	In 1883, Augusta Stowe Gullen, only daughter of Emily Howard Stowe, became the first woman to graduate from a Canadian medical school.
159	9-11	Unidentified newspaper clipping, Augusta Stowe-Gullen, "Stowe Scrapbooks."

CHAPTER EIGHT

page	line	source
162	5,6	Bernard Hoodless, "Address" on the twenty-fifth anniversary of Macdonald College, 1928.
162	8-11	Ruth Howes, "Adelaide Hoodless: Woman with a Vision," *The Clear Spirit*, p. 7.
162	35-36	Elsie MacGill, *My Mother the Judge*, p. 45.

Emily Murphy

The biographical sketch of Emily Murphy is drawn largely from assorted newspaper stories, "Five Persons from Alberta" by Eleanor Harman, and *Emily Murphy: Crusader* by Byrne Hope Sanders.

Unless otherwise specified, short quotes are taken from *Emily Murphy: Crusader*. Extracts and additional references are listed below:

page	line	source
165	29ff	Emily Murphy, "The Woman's Court," *Maclean's Magazine,* January, 1920.
165		For a report of the "Person's Case" see Eleanor Harman, "Five Persons from Alberta" in *The Clear Spirit.*
169	4-13	Sanders, *Emily Murphy: Crusader,* p. 241.
174	27-32	Emily Murphy, *Janey Canuck in the West,* p. 138.
175	11-13	*Ibid.,* p. 208.
175	18-22	*Ibid.,* p. 213.
175	28-29	Sanders, *Emily Murphy: Crusader,* p. 108.
175	36ff	Murphy, *Janey Canuck in the West,* p. 224.
176	11-17	Sanders, *Emily Murphy: Crusader,* p. 132.
176	23-29; 33-35	*Ibid.,* p. 133-4.
177	29-33	Murphy, *The Black Candle,* p. 1.
178	3-20	*Ibid.,* p. 29.
178	25-29	*Ibid.,* p. 7.
178	31-34	Sanders, *Emily Murphy: Crusader,* p. 150.
179	7-11	*Ibid.,* p. 148.
180	15-19	*Ibid.,* p. 256.
180	31-32	*Ibid.,* p. 258.

CHAPTER NINE

page	line	source
184	23ff	See Jean LeMoyne, "La Femme dans la Civilization," *Convergences,* pp. 70-100.
184	32	See Ramsay Cook, "The Ideology of Survival," *Canada and the French Canadian Question,* pp. 79-103.
185	8	Brother Jérôme, *Les Insolences du Frère Untel,* pp. 55, 67, 83, 84.

Claire Martin

Unless otherwise specified, all quotes attributed to Claire Martin are taken from her autobiography. Extracts and additional references are listed below.

page	line	source
186	1	Claire Martin is the pen name of Mme. Roland Faucher who is presently living in France.
186	3-4	Claire Martin, *In an Iron Glove.* (Originally published in French in two volumes *Dans un gant de Fer* and *La Joue Droite,* Montreal: Le Circle du Livre de France Ltee, 1965, 1966.)
187	37ff	Barry Callaghan, "Woman in an Iron Glove," *Telegram,* February 1, 1960.
192	18ff	Claire Martin, Interview with Barry Callaghan and Helen Hutchison, *CBC Radio,* July, 1972.

Thérèse Casgrain

The biographical portrait of Thérèse Casgrain is based largely on an interview with her in Montreal in 1974, on the many newspaper and magazine articles on her, and on her autobiography *Woman in a Man's World.*

Unless otherwise specified, quotations are taken from *Woman in a Man's World.* Additional sources and references for extracts are listed below.

page	line	source
193	21-24	Thérèse Casgrain, Interview.
194	4-5	*Ibid.*
194	24	The Comité provincial pour le Suffrage féminin was not the first women's suffrage organization in Quebec but rather an improved version of what had been the Montreal Suffrage Association, an association formed in 1913 but disbanded in 1919 when its members realized that an English-speaking organization could make little headway in a French-speaking province.
195	25-31	L. Perrin, Curé of Notre Dame. Letter published in *La Semaine Réligieuse,* December 9, 1921.
196	16-17	Margaret Gould, *Star,* November 9, 1937.
201	37ff	Casgrain, Interview.
203	27-29	Margaret Aitken, *The Telegram,* November 14, 1953.
204	15-16	Margaret Aitken, *The Globe and Mail,* August 31, 1955.
204	30-31	Casgrain, Interview.

Bibliography

Aitken, Margaret. *The Telegram.* Toronto: November 14, 1953.
———. *The Globe and Mail.* Toronto: August 31, 1955.
Allen, Richard. *The Social Passion: Religion and Social Reform in Canada, 1914-28.* Toronto: University of Toronto Press, 1971.
A Member of the Community. *The Life and Letters of Rev. Mother Dease.* Toronto: McClelland & Stewart, 1916.
Anderson, Margaret. *Mother Was Not A Person.* Montreal: Content Pub. Ltd. & Black Rose books, 1972.
Bannerman, Jean. *One Hundred Leading Ladies. Leading Ladies-Canada, 1639-1967.* Dundas, Ontario: Carrsood, 1967.
Berton, Laura Beatrice. *I Married The Klondike.* Toronto: McClelland & Stewart, 1954.
Berton, Pierre, *The Klondike Fever.* New York: Alfred Knopf, 1958.
Binnie-Clark, Georgina. *Wheat and Women.* Toronto: Bell & Cockburn, 1914.
Bird, Isabella Lucy. *The English Woman in America.* London: John Murray, 1956. Reprint. Toronto: University of Toronto Press, 1966.
Black, Martha (Mrs. George). *My Seventy Years.* As told to Elizabeth Bailey Price. Toronto: Thomas Nelson & Sons Ltd., 1938.
———. *Diary.* February 1937.
———. "Empire Study-The Yukon, Past and Present." *Echoes,* Autumn 1945.
Bompas, Charlotte Selina (Cox). *A Heroine of the North. Memories of Charlotte Selina Bompas (1830-1917), wife of the First Bishop of Selkirk (Yukon).* Compiled by S. A. Archer. Toronto: Macmillan, 1929.
Bradley, Mrs. Mary. *A Narrative of the Life and Christian Experience of Mrs. Mary Bradley of St. John, N.B.* Boston: Strong & Brodhead, 1849.

Buchanon, Ruth. *My Mother*. Toronto: Mundy-Goodfellow Printing Co. for Women's Missionary Society of the Presbyterian Church, 1938.

Bullock, Rev. William. *The Ruler's Daughter Raised*. A funeral discourse on the occasion of the death of Miss Bliss. Halifax: 1851.

Burkholder, Mabel Grace. *"Kit" Life of Kathleen Blake Colman*. Niagara Falls: Evening Review, 1933.

Burwash, Rev. Nathaniel. *Memorials of the Life of Edward & Lydia Jackson*. Toronto: Rose, 1876.

Callaghan, Barry. "Woman in an Iron Glove." *The Telegram*. Toronto: February 1, 1960.

Canada Law Journal XXXIII:4 (February 16, 1897).

Carter, C. A. and Bailey, T. M. *The Diary of Sophia Macnab*. Hamilton: W. L. Griffin Ltd., 1968.

Casgrain, Thérèse. *A Woman in a Man's World*. Toronto: McClelland & Stewart, 1972.

Casgrain, Thérèse. Interview. Montreal: November 16, 1974.

Chapman, Ethel. "Adelaide Hoodless." *Pioneers in Adult Education,* edited by Harriet Rouillard. Toronto: Thomas Nelson & Sons, 1953.

Clark, S. D. *The Developing Canadian Community*. Toronto: University of Toronto Press, 1962.

Cleverdon, Catherine. *The Women's Suffrage Movement in Canada*. Introduction by Ramsay Cook. Toronto: University of Toronto Press, 1974 (copyright Canada, 1950).

Clint, M. B. *Our Bit. Memories of War Service by A Canadian Nursing Sister*. Montreal: Barwick Ltd., 1934.

Collins, Alice Helen (Roger). *Pen Pictures ... Real People, Sketches No. V, VI, VII, VIII. Elizabeth Veals; Peter McArthur; Ellen Mary Knox; J. L Yule*. Walkerton: Herald-Times, 1935.

Cook, Ramsay. *Canada and the French Canadian Question*. Toronto: Macmillan, 1966.

Day, Effie Jamieson. *Annie Elizabeth Bradley*. Toronto: Women's Missionary Society of the United Church of Canada, 1936.

Eggleston, Wilfrid. "Nellie McClung: Crusader." *Canadian Author and Bookman* 19 (September 1943): 21.

Ellen Mary Knox. A Memorial Volume. Toronto: Havergal College, 1925.

Faucher, Mme Roland (Claire Martin). *In an Iron Glove*. Translated by Philip Statford. Toronto: Ryerson Press, 1968.

Fenton, Faith. *Montreal Daily Witness,* Saturday, November 27, 1897.

Franklin, Stephen. "Ma Murray: Fighting Editor." *Weekend Magazine* 8:23.

French, Doris. *High Button Boot Straps: Federation of Women Teachers' Associations of Ontario, 1918-1968*. Toronto: Ryerson Press, 1968.

Gaudin, Samuel. *Forty-Four Years with the Northern Cree*. Toronto: Published for the author by Mundy-Goodfellow Printing Co. Ltd., 1942.

————. "Letters to the Mission Board. 1890-1920." Property of Victoria College Archives, University of Toronto.

Gibbon, John M. in collaboration with Mathewson, Mary S. *Three Centuries of Canadian Nursing*. Toronto: Macmillan, 1947.

Gillen, Mollie. "Maud Montgomery: the girl who wrote Green Gables," in *Chatelaine* 46 (July 1973):7, p. 40.

Goggin, Superintendent. *Proceedings.* Dominion Educational Association, (47) 1904, p. 39.

Gould, Margaret. *Star.* Toronto: November 9, 1937.

Gullen, F. C. "Gullen History." Manuscript scrapbook of Stowe, Lossing, and Gullen families. Archives, Victoria College, Toronto.

Hacker, Carlotta. *The Indomitable Lady Doctors.* Toronto: Clarke Irwin & Co. Ltd., 1974.

Haig, Kennethe M. *Brave Harvest.* Toronto: Thomas Allen, Ltd., 1945.

Hansard. First session Eighteenth Parliament, 1936.

Harman, Eleanor. "Five Persons from Alberta" in *The Clear Spirit,* edited by Mary Quayle Innis. Toronto: University of Toronto Press, 1967.

Henderson, Mary (Gillespie). *Memories of My Early Years.* Montreal: Charters & Charters, 1937.

Heward, S. A. and Wallace, W. S. *An American Lady in Old Toronto: The Letters of Julia Lambert, 1821-1854.* Ottawa: Royal Society of Canada, 1946.

Holt, Miss C. E. *An Autobiographical Sketch of a Teacher's Life.* Quebec: Carrel, 1875.

Hoodless, Bernard. "Address," on the twenty-fifth anniversary of Macdonald College, 1928.

House, Jackson. "Ma Murray: Salty Scourge of Lillooet." *Maclean's Magazine* 79 (March 19, 1966).

Howes, Ruth. "Adelaide Hoodless: Woman with a Vision" in *The Clear Spirit,* edited by Mary Quayle Innis. Toronto: University of Toronto Press, 1967.

Hughes, James L. *Equal Suffrage.* Toronto: 1895.

Innis, Mary Quayle. *Clear Spirit: Twenty Canadian Women and their Times.* Toronto: University of Toronto Press, 1967.

Brother Jérôme, *Les Insolences du Frère Untel.* Montreal: Editions de L'homme, 1960.

Johnson, Mrs. Amelia B. *A Brief Memoir and Letters of Amelia, Annie, and Thomas Johnson.* Toronto: Hunter, Rose & Co., 1888.

Johnston, Jean. *Wilderness Women.* Toronto: Peter Martin Associates Ltd., 1973.

Keddell, Georgina. *The Newspapering Murrays.* Toronto: McClelland & Stewart, 1967. Revised edition. Lillooet: Lillooet Publishers, 1974.

Kell, Mrs. J. A. C. Telephone Interview. Owen Sound: December, 1973.

Kell, Rev. Dr. J. A. C. Interview. Toronto: December, 1973.

Kells, Edna. *Elizabeth McDougall.* Toronto: The United Church Publishing House, (no date).

Klinck, Carl F. *Literary History of Canada.* Toronto: University of Toronto Press, 1967.

Koedt, A., Levine, E., Rapone, A. *Radical Feminism.* New York: Quadrangle Books, 1973.

Laing, Margaret. *Woman on Woman.* London: Sidgwick & Jackson, 1971.

Lambert, Norman P. "A Joan of the West." *Canadian Magazine* 46(January 1916):265-268.

LeMoyne, Jean. *Convergences,* Montreal: Editions HMH, 1969.

Lucia, Ellis. *Klondike Kate: The Life and Legend of Kitty Rockwell.* New York: Hastings House Pub., 1962.

Macdonald, Eva Mader. "A Survey of Women Physicians in Canada." *Cana-*

dian *Medical Association Journal* 94 (June 4, 1966):1223-1227.

MacDermot, Dr. H. E. *The Nursing School of the Montreal General Hospital.* Montreal: The Alumni Association, 1940.

MacDermot, Hugh Ernest. *Maude Abbott: A Memoir.* Toronto: Macmillan, 1941.

MacGill, Elsie. *My Mother the Judge.* Toronto: Ryerson Press, 1955.

———. Interview. Toronto: May 1974.

MacGill, Helen Gregory. "Women Have Not Failed in Politics." *Liberty Magazine* 13 (May 1936):20.

MacNaughton, Katherine, F.C. *The Development of the Theory and Practice of Education in New Brunswick,* 1947.

Marshall, Joyce. Introduction to *Word from New France. The Selected Letters of Marie de l'Incarnation.* Toronto: Oxford University Press, 1967.

McClung, Marcia. Interview. Toronto: March 20, 1973.

McClung, Nellie. *Clearing in the West.* New York: Fleming H. Revell Co., 1936.

———. *In Times Like These.* 1915. Reprint. Introduction by Veronica Strong-Boag. Toronto: University of Toronto Press, 1972.

———. Foreword to *The Next of Kin.* Boston and New York: Houghton Miffon Co., 1917.

———. *The Stream Runs Fast.* Toronto: Thomas Allen, 1945.

McKay, Madelaine. Tape by an Indian woman at Cross Lake who knew Anna Gaudin. Cross Lake: 1973.

McKinney, J. Willard. *Louise C, McKinney.* London, Ontario: Dominion Literature Depository, (n.d.).

Melancon, Rev. J.M. *Life of Mother Marie Rose (1801-49).* Montreal:Therien Freres, 1930.

Murphy, Emily, *Janey Canuck in the West.* Toronto: J. M. Dent & Sons, 1915. Reprint. Toronto: McClelland & Stewart, 1975.

———. *Seeds of Pine* (Janey Canuck). Toronto: Musson Book Co., 1912.

———. *The Black Candle.* Toronto: Thomas Allen, 1922.

———. "The Woman's Court." *Maclean's Magazine,* January 1920, p. 27.

Murray, Margaret. Telephone interview. Lillooet, B.C.: February 12, 1974.

———. Letter to author. March 1974.

Patterson, Rev. George, *Memoirs of the Rev. S. F. Johnston, The Rev. J. W. Matheson and Mrs. Mary Johnston Matheson. Missionaries of Tanna.* Philadelphia: Martien, 1864.

Pearce, Lorne, in *The Royal Commission on Book Publishing.* Edited by Richard Rohmer, Dalton Camp, Marsh Jenneret. Toronto: Queen's Printer, 1972.

Phillips, C. E. *The Development of Education in Canada.* Toronto: W. J. Gage & Co. Ltd., 1957.

Proceedings, *Dominion Educational Association,* (47) 1904, p. 39.

Randleson, Sarah. *Just One Blue Bonnet: The Life Story of Ada Florence Kinton.* Toronto: William Briggs, 1907.

Ravenhill, Alice. *Alice Ravenhill, The Memoirs of an Educational Pioneer.* Toronto: Dent, 1951.

Ridley, Hilda, M. *A Synopsis of Women Suffrage in Canada.* n.d., n.p.

Roberts, Sarah Ellen. *Of Us and Oxen. A True Tale of Pioneering in Alberta Around the Turn of the Century.* Saskatoon: Modern Press, 1968.

Roper, Gordon. "New Forces: New Fiction" in *The Literary History of Canada.* Toronto: University of Toronto Press, 1967.

Ross, Mrs. Esther. Telephone interviews. Winnipeg: January 1974.

Rowles, Edith. *Home Economics in Canada.* Saskatoon: University of Saskatoon Press, 1964.

Royal Commission on Book Publishing. Toronto: Queen's Printer and Publisher, 1972.

Royal Commission on the Status of Women. Florence Bird, Chairman, Ottawa: Queen's Printer, 1970.

Rugoff, Milton. *Prudery and Passion: Sexuality in Victorian America.* London: Rupert Hart-Davis, 1972.

Salverson, Laura Goodman. *Confessions of an Immigrant's Daughter.* Toronto: Ryerson Press, 1939.

Sanders, Byrne Hope. *Emily Murphy, Crusader.* Toronto: Macmillan, 1945.

———. *Famous Women.* Toronto: Clarke Irwin, 1958.

Scriver, Jessie Boyd. "Maude E. Abbott" in *The Clear Spirit,* edited by Mary Quayle Innis. Toronto: University of Toronto Press, 1967.

Shand, Margaret Clark and Shand, Ora M. *The Summit and Beyond.* Caldwell, Idaho: The Claxton Printers, 1959.

Shaw, R. L. *Proud Heritage.* Toronto: Ryerson Press, 1957.

Shipley, Nan. *Anna and the Indians.* Toronto: Ryerson Press, 1955.

Skelton, Isabel. *The Backwoods Woman: A Chronicle of Pioneer Home Life in Upper and Lower Canada.* Toronto: Ryerson Press, 1924.

Smith-Shortt, Elizabeth. "Historical Sketch of Medical Education of Women in Kingston." Paper read before the Osler Club, Queen's University, September 14, 1916.

Stephanson, Mary Lee, ed. *Women in Canada.* Toronto: New Press, 1973.

Stowe-Gullen, Augusta. "Stowe Scrapbook No. 3 and 4." *Stowe Collection,* Sir Wilfrid Laurier University, Kitchener.

Strange, Kathleen. *With the West in Her Eyes.* Toronto: Macmillan, 1945.

Strong-Boag, V. Introduction to *In Times Like These* by Nellie McClung. Toronto: University of Toronto Press, 1967.

Thomas, Eileen Mitchell. "Sisters-in-Law." *Law Society of Upper Canada Commemorative Issue* VI (December 1972).

Thompson, J. "The Influence of Dr. Emily Stowe on the Woman Suffrage Movement in Canada." *Ontario History*, December 1962.

Tivy, Louis. *Your Loving Anna, Letters from the Ontario Frontier.* Toronto: University of Toronto Press, 1972.

Van Steen, Marcus. "A Voice that Cried in the Wilderness." *Weekend Magazine, The Globe and Mail,* February 27, 1960.

Wilson, Rev. Robert. *Piety Portrayed in the Lives and Death of Mr. and Mrs. Burpee of Sheffield, New Brunswick.* St. John, N.B.: H. Chubb & Co., 1870.

Wooldridge, Helen. "No Place for a Lady." Play on Clara Brett Martin tentatively scheduled on CBC Radio for November 1, 1975.

Youman's, Letitia. *Campaign Echoes.* Toronto: Wm. Briggs, 1893.

Young, Scott. *The Globe and Mail.* Toronto: January 9, 1968.

Zieman, Margaret. "Nellie Was a Lady Terror." *Maclean's Magazine.* 66 (October 1, 1953):20-21, 62-66.